ELEV∧TED

Martha,

ELEV∧TED

TAKE YOUR LIFE TO THE
NEXT LEVEL

I am so grateful for our journey together. Here's to your brave journey ahead! Love,

KIMBERLY NAPIER

Print paperback ISBN: 978-1-7355695-2-9

Cover Design: Chris Winders

Editing: Elizabeth Exline

Interior Design and Formatting: E.M. Tippetts Book Designs

Author's photo courtesy of: Gigi DeManio Photography

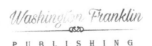

Washington Franklin

P U B L I S H I N G

This book is dedicated to all my loves,
Kasey, Jenna, Devin, Emilio and Ron, who
inspire me to be my best every day.

And to my golden angels, Chase and Daisy, who
hold the space for me to do so.

ADVANCE PRAISE

"*Elevated* answers the age old question of "now what"? We have all been there, finished a retreat or a course and feel excited and elevated but then we have the crash. Kimberly walks you through the process of staying in an elevated state, a higher frequency from which you can work and live your life."

—Madisyn Taylor, Cofounder, DailyOM

"This is a very special book – a book born out of experience and deep emotional intelligence.

Who wouldn't love to learn how to have a daily, effective practice to elevate your life in a simple but effective way? I felt myself being uplifted and supported as I read Kimberly's words.

This is not only a lovely read, but is full of exceptional guidance, encouragement and direction!"

—Rosie Dalton, National Speaker,
Retreat Facilitator, and Spiritual Coach.

"*Elevated* is not only a guide for our times, it's a personal handbook for everyone. Kimberly's honesty and authentic writing in this gem of a book will keep you turning pages. The information here is real, attainable and totally inspiring. It will help you understand more of the truth of who you are and who you have always been. You will want to keep it by your side, in your bag with you during the day and by your bed at night."

—Katherine Glass, Owner of Healing
Essence Center, Psychic, Medium,
Healer, Spiritual Teacher.

"This book touches upon many highly complex consciousness topics in a way that makes them relatable.... to open the door to a greater understanding of what's possible in our human experiences. If you've been looking for a jumping off point into putting these spiritual concepts into action in your life, look no further. By sharing examples from her clients as well as drawing from her own soul growth journey, this book will provide you a smorgasbord of ideas to open up to what's waiting for you once you tap into the power that lies within you."

—Erika Elmuts, Quantum healer, Channeler and
Consciousness Mentor.

"This isn't hocus pocus. This is the real deal. When we fall from Grace, this books reminds us to remember who we are and straighten our crowns! We all have a seat in the thrown of this beautiful kingdom called life and Kimberly reminds us how to remain calm, in control of our emotions and elevate our existence."

—Erin DiCarlo Founder,
President of DoveTail Companies

"This book is amazing! It's so profound, yet so easy to comprehend and implement! With experience as her teacher, Kimberly has created a masterful manual to help anyone learn to lead a more elevated, conscious existence."

—Janelle Salzman, Reiki Master,
Biomagnetism Practitioner, Ayurvedic Practitioner

" In *Elevated - Take Your Life to the Next Level*, Kimberly helps to demystify some of the greatest truths in life. We all know that feeling of being around someone that is peaceful, graceful and "high vibration." Kimberly helps to unlock the steps to become that person ourselves. What separates this book from others is that Kimberly is vulnerable herself. She weaves her personal story throughout and you can see how she has overcome some rather large and painful obstacles in her own life. She has authentically walked her life path and devised a system and methodology to achieve and maintain a high vibration way of living. Thank you Kimberly, for writing yet another amazing book that will remain on my bookshelf for reference for years to come."

—Kathleen Katterhagen, Author of *Invest in Hope: Your healing portfolio for extraordinary results.*

CONTENTS

ACKNOWLEDGEMENTS

This is not the first book I've ever written, but in many ways, it was an entirely new process. And honoring the process – which was at once intense and messy, uncertain and rewarding – could not have been possible without the presence and support of the following people.

I have to thank my girls, Kasey and Jenna. I am so grateful to be your mom, and I am so proud of who you are and who you are becoming. Thank you for your patience and for your love and acceptance of me – that "weird mom" in town. I love you both with all of my heart.

To my husband, Ron. Thank you for continuing to hold me to my highest standards of who I want to be in this world. I am blessed by your love and belief in me, and I am excited for our journey forward. We have so much to create together!

Thank you to my business partner and soul-sister, Katherine Glass. You taught me all I know about the energy field. Your example of intentional living combined with playful energy is a model each of us should follow. I am grateful for our laughter, support and creation together.

To my sister, Chris. Thank you for always bringing me back to my center when it counts. I will forever appreciate your love and guidance. You balance me, and your unconditional love and support give me wings.

To my loyal friend, Natalie Kattwinkel. I treasure our connection and friendship. Thank you for always listening and offering unwavering help and expertise when needed.

To all of my clients who inspired me to write this book. You call me forward every day to show up fully. I hope you find in this book insight, inspiration and the freedom to live with greater ease.

Thank you to Joy Stone for being a constant with me on this journey of fellowship, friendship and entrepreneurship. Having each other's backs is a godsend.

To Chase and Daisy for always holding space for me and raising my vibration through your unconditional and loving presence. I could not have written this book without you. We did this together!

PREFACE

First and foremost, I wrote this book to help my clients on their journey forward. After we complete our work, my clients often ask, "Now what? How do I stay on this path?" This book is designed to help them and you stay on your conscious path forward. I write to help give people a roadmap for living a better life, and I only share ideas and tools that have helped me and my clients.

I am not a guru, expert, Ph.D., yoga teacher, therapist or even a writer (at least not by trade!). I am a certified life coach and intuitive medium who has helped hundreds of people create conscious and fulfilling lives on their terms. I am also a lifelong researcher and learner, and I know I am called to wake up people from living on autopilot.

In my first book, "Know What You Want Next," I share more about my own wake-up call after losing my husband, Sean, to suicide. That experience changed my life forever, but the most remarkable change came from within. When your world turns upside down, it is easy to give yourself permission to do things differently. It is much harder to make a change when life is going along "just fine."

I am here to share with you that there is more than "fine" in this life. No matter what your circumstances, you can choose to live a more empowered and elevated life.

I have experienced the joys, gifts, challenges and lessons that come from choosing an unconventional path. If you also crave greater connection to yourself and your spiritual path, this book is the guide you need. The path forward won't always be linear, mainstream or predictable, but it *will* be uplifting, confronting (at times) and 100% worthwhile.

I hope this book helps more people like you create a conscious world and live in the ripples of greater collective consciousness.

INTRODUCTION

This book is an invitation to live your life more consciously and, in so doing, elevate your life (as well as those of the people around you) to the next level. I will share how to do this sustainably so that you can not only reach that higher state of consciousness but stay there to live fully and mindfully in a soul-centered way. That is, in essence, an elevated life.

I wrote this book as a sequel to "Know What You Want Next," which is about how to create positive change and get clear about the next step in your life. It was inspired by my own life's reinvention after a tragic wake-up call – the suicide of my first husband. I published that book right before we entered what became another tragic wake-up call for many: the pandemic of 2020. "Know What You Want Next" served as a roadmap for many during that time as they reassessed what they really wanted. Truth be told, I also relied on that book to help me maintain a positive mindset during such uncertain times.

It turns out that uncertain times are actually a good time to grow and, yes, write. I began working on this book as I practiced my own skills for staying in a higher vibration and level of consciousness, even as the intense world outside of me affected my energy field. I was able to apply so much of what I learned to keep myself grounded in spite of the chaos around me, and I was able to help my clients do the same. I realized just how powerful these teachings were that I felt compelled to share them here.

So, while "Know What You Want Next" is the roadmap to your future, "Elevated" is the formula to stay in the flow of conscious living and continued upleveling.

This book is also a practical, how-to application of the principles around the levels of consciousness that were informed by the research of David Hawkins, M.D., Ph.D. (Hawkins introduced these concepts in his book, "Power vs. Force.") You will learn what specific emotional states do to your well-being and energy field, and how to shift your vibrational state. The insights you'll glean here are sticky, meaning that they are so clear and profound that your rational mind will glom onto them and remember them. In fact, I was so blown away when I first encountered Hawkins' work several years ago that I started to teach it to my clients and in my workshops. I honestly feel that it has been some of the most compelling and potentially life-altering work done in our lifetime.

My goal with this book is to help you get where you truly want and deserve to be in your life. I have created a holistic process that I call KARMA to help you do just that. This process incorporates multiple tools to help you manage your thoughts, beliefs, actions, emotional state and energy field, which ultimately allows you to be intentional about raising your state of consciousness. We will also explore how abundance blocks can keep you from realizing your potential.

Interestingly, as you do the work laid out in the following pages, you may find that what you thought you wanted is not what you want at all anymore – or perhaps you want a simplified, elevated version. I guarantee that much will be revealed to you during the process.

What you will also find as you gradually raise your state of consciousness is that life moves with greater ease and flow, and your manifestations happen almost instantly. What is for you will find you more quickly. You will move with more fluidity and grace through your life. And when you fall, as we all do, you will recover faster. (I will share how to do that too – and I admit I am still learning.)

My wish is that we all choose to live more consciously, not only to raise the state of our own being, but to elevate that of our beautiful planet, too. As you will see in the pages that follow, if we each do our small part, we can significantly impact and elevate the world we live in. Thanks for coming on this journey with me. We are all just walking each other home...

1
PINCH ME!

"I'll have what she's having."
—When Harry Met Sally

remember boarding the plane to Rome with my new husband, the man of my dreams. *Pinch me!* I thought. *Is this real?* There I was, in first class with my soulmate, drinking champagne and syncing our monitors to watch *Grease* (yes, *Grease*) together as we jetted off to Rome and then Santorini for a week of bliss without kids, clients or interruptions. We had just returned from Hawaii, where we had gotten "Maui'd" as my husband playfully called it with our four kids. We were a modern-day Brady bunch – me and my girls, him and his boys and a fairytale wedding – all of it part of a beautiful, intentional step-by-step manifestation.

Elevated

I was on cloud nine (pun intended!) as we headed off on our five-star honeymoon to create our new life together. *Nothing can change this feeling*, I thought. *Nothing can bring me down!*

Or so I believed.

I truly manifested that moment and getting there. It had been a dream that became my reality through the intentions, visualizations, beliefs and actions I focused on. When we arrived in Santorini, we both had that déjà vu moment: We looked at each other and almost on cue said we'd been there before. Together.

We both had dreamed of Santorini even before we met. I meditated about it as my happy place, and my husband fantasized about going there every morning when he glanced at his calendar of Santorini photography. Ironically, we were both alone while we were doing this. Me, recently widowed, and he, recently divorced. When we shared this dream with each other (within days of meeting each other!), neither of us could believe it was true. And when we finally got to Santorini, there were no more doubts. We knew we had each found a lost soulmate. We indeed had been together before.

Moments like that remind you there is a greater power or force at work.

Pinch Me!

We had found each other on our new paths and created a new circle together. All of the inner work we did on ourselves prior to meeting made us a vibrational match for each other at that point in time, and we felt truly blessed.

My life had transformed dramatically over the course of a couple years following Sean's passing. I went from a hellish situation to one that was beyond my dreams. This didn't just happen to me of course. I was the catalyst in lifting myself from the depths of hell to the gates of heaven. I share a lot of that journey in my first book, "Know What You Want Next."

Since you are reading this book, however, you probably already understand that you can create your own reality. Your thoughts, your intentions and your actions shape the world that you live in. No matter what is happening on the outside, you can master yourself to manage who you are inside and what you attract on the outside. This is exactly what I did to attain my level of happiness and bliss.

Is a state of elevated bliss sustainable though? Can you or I or anybody stay in that honeymoon state forever? And if so, how? That is what I hope to answer in this book. I want to share with you how you can help yourself sustain a blissful, elevated state. And if you fall out of it, I want to show you how to get back there faster.

But first, why should you trust me? I mean, my life looks pretty spectacular right now based on what you just read, right? It must be easy for me to just stay in an elevated state all the time given what I am capable of manifesting, right? Wrong. I had a big fall from bliss when I got back to reality.

Truth is, I manifested another dream come true that greeted me as soon as I got back from my honeymoon. My bliss was cut short. But the silver lining was that I learned so much about myself, my process and how to raise my level of consciousness to avoid future pitfalls that I can share with you what to do, and what not to do, to remain the master of your reality.

When I returned from my honeymoon, rather than return to my family, I went to assist in teaching a course in positive psychology at Kripalu with my mentor. This was a big deal for me and not something I could pass up, although in hindsight perhaps I should have. Don't get me wrong: It was an amazing experience and something that I deeply wanted, but the timing was not ideal, and I do believe my ego and fear of missing out got the better of me.

Pinch Me!

When I first went to Kripalu, I was grieving Sean. My certification in positive psychology helped me and my girls heal and thrive going forward. Certainly, I wanted to share these gifts with others, and that is why I became a coach. To be able to teach side-by-side with my mentor was the validation I needed that I was where I was supposed to be. However, I do not think I was mentally prepared for what was to come. I walked in hopeful, excited, expansive and blissful, forgetting that those who met me were not in that state I had worked so hard to attain. Instead, they were where I had been just a few years earlier – feeling hopeless, powerless, defeated in some ways and wanting to find a new way forward.

While my high vibration at the time could uplift others, I needed to meet them where they were. This was not what I was ready for, nor was it really what my soul wanted in that moment. Deep down, I knew I was meant to be home with my family, creating our new nest and allowing myself to experience the bliss. But my fear of missing out, my eagerness to please others and my desire to teach at Kripalu no matter what drove me to stay. My ego was really calling the shots.

Throughout my time there, I felt myself losing ground and getting lost in grief like I was reliving my first Kripalu experience. I started to feel myself falling down what I call the "shame well." Old stories, fears and regretful moments I thought I had made peace with flooded me. Surely there was more for me to process and more to learn, but that was not the time. I wondered if I had taken on too much too soon. I had to work extra hard to ground myself and clear what I was experiencing so that I could hold space for others. While that was possible, I felt like I was dismissing my truth in the process.

I left feeling affirmed in my path but exhausted, depleted and icky. My colleague has the perfect phrase for this feeling of having your personal energy coopted: Getting slimed. While I felt so good about the work I had done helping others, I had nothing left to give to my family when I got home – or to myself for that matter. It was like all the bliss in me was wiped out.

I ultimately learned how we can give away our energy, power and light without consciously deciding to. In addition to understanding that I had limits and needed (and deserved) better boundaries, I realized I had to figure out how to bounce back quickly. I had so much waiting for me at home: my kids, my new husband and boys, my fur babies and my clients.

Pinch Me!

It took me weeks, maybe months, to replenish and energetically get back to where I was after Santorini. I revisited all of the tools I had used before to get me to a higher state of being, and I vowed never to deplete myself like that again. I needed to deepen my learning about energy protection and healing as well as how to manage my own vibration to influence my state of consciousness.

The only thing I could manifest from the state I was in after Kripalu was more mess and chaos. Of course, this put me back in the throes of being a student again. I learned as much as I could about energy, vibration and the levels of consciousness. And for the past several years, I've practiced, experimented and taught what I've learned.

I have studied how to work with my vibration to manifest and create stability in a higher, elevated state of consciousness. A greater test of this learning occurred for me and my clients (well, all of us really) during the 2020 pandemic. While the world was full of uncertainty and despair, staying grounded in a higher state was possible – and for many of my clients, it became their new, albeit challenging, way forward.

What I want to share with you is a formula to help you master your vibration so that you can manifest more of what you want and less of what you don't on a consistent basis. So that you can stay elevated, no matter what is happening around you.

2
RISING UP

"Worry is using your imagination to create what you don't want."
—Esther Hicks

Mindfulness, manifesting, higher states of consciousness … these were not concepts I learned growing up. I often joke that if there had been a mantra in my house growing up, it would've been, "Life's not fair." Underscoring that perspective was a state of near-constant anxiety, worrying being something that was instilled in me early on. My mom would actually say, "I need something new to worry about," as if she were consciously looking for new things to worry about as other things were crossed off the list. I observed and eventually adopted this attitude, looking for new worries as I moved forward in my life.

Elevated

Worry is a fear-state to somehow help you feel in control. As a young girl, I relied on worry to help me not get my hopes up, but worry really solidified its presence in my life when I was 7 years old. My family was staying at my friend's house in Cape Cod. Her parents were recently divorced, and my mom had rented the house from them for a week. I was so excited to be there and spend that time with my sister and my family. I can actually use the word "giddy" to describe it. I remember the moment I said to my mom I was so happy to be there, and that my parents were married and not divorced like my friend's. My mom used that very moment to tell me that she and my dad were actually getting divorced! I was blindsided. I had no idea they were even considering divorce. It created so many worries within me about what would happen to us and to me.

I felt so caught off guard that it triggered a protective mechanism in me not to trust things as they appeared. I see now that I used worry as a protective shield. I started to believe that if I worried about something and thought the worst might happen, then somehow things would be OK and I wouldn't be disappointed or blindsided again.

I call this my worry wound, and it led me to lower my expectations in a lot of areas of my life. It also become a motivator for me. Worry can drive you: If you worry that you won't be enough, or aren't worthy of what you have or want, you will do anything to get that next thing. Much of my corporate success I owe to my worry wound and feeling of unworthiness. It helped me achieve and accumulate more than I had originally set out to for sure.

It wasn't until my world was turned upside down by Sean's suicide (again, blindsided) that I found myself with real worries that were so overwhelming, I learned the art of surrender. Ironically, when one of your worst fears comes true, you just don't worry as much going forward. At least this was my experience. Everything after that moment became eligible for comparison to what I had already been through, and nothing could be as bad as that.

On some level, I also felt like I was owed divine compensation for what I had been through. A crazy interpretation of karma, but that was how I rationalized it in my brain. The worst was behind me, I thought.

Unconsciously, I became somewhat numb and less attached to outcomes around me. It was a weird form of self-preservation. I started to see how, if I didn't worry about something, somehow it worked itself out. I instinctively started to unlearn worrying as I became more focused on living my life day by day, moment by moment.

I didn't have a term or a plan for it, but I was learning what it meant to be truly present.

Manifesting was next. I discovered pretty quickly that my mood influenced what I experienced that day. I often refer to this as "The George Costanza Effect." When George from *Seinfeld* did everything the opposite of his usual one day, he received everything he ever wanted. I played with this concept in little ways and then ultimately in big ways, and I felt its immediate effects.

At first, I tried doing things the opposite way, like acting as if my life were working out the way I wanted. I practiced this by nudging myself to go out of my comfort zone, which, in the early days of grief, was just getting dressed and going to the grocery store. I would act how a "normal" person would act (one who was not grieving). It was like I was playing a part in a play where I didn't have to be a "poor thing" anymore. It felt freeing. I would act how I wanted to feel. I would smile and talk to people in a curious and thoughtful way, and I noticed quickly this way of being helped me to attract exactly what I was putting out there. One day, out of the blue, a woman offered to buy my whole basket of items. She said she just wanted too because she liked my energy. This was manifesting at its core.

Rising Up

Back to George. The only trouble for George was that he could not stay in this high receiving place. In fact, he ultimately lost most everything – he couldn't stay in a high enough dominant vibration to maintain it.

Manifesting is a state we are always in. We are just not always conscious of it. Once you become conscious of it, you can manifest a sh*tstorm just as easily as you can a dream. The power is in your recovery (if you manifest something negative) and in you choosing the dominant frequency you want to emit.

Why is this? Well, yes, it is your positive thoughts and clarity. But more important than that is your energetic vibration. Everything in the universe is energy, so everything has a vibrational frequency. Your vibrational frequency attracts what matches your energy.

You can see this play out in everyday life. If you greet someone with a smile, you know you will have a more pleasant experience with them than if you show disgust or complain. You will attract the energy back no matter what you put out. I started to notice that whenever I would be open and cheerful versus closed and fearful I would receive more of what I was putting out there. In fact, the more expansive and open I was, the more good stuff came my way in the form of connections, opportunities and synchronicities, and even my soulmate.

The key to manifesting, however, is not always taught in the New Age realm and it is this: Positive thinking is not enough. In actuality, you have to *be it to receive it* – and especially to sustain it. You can't fake your vibration. This means you have to learn how to master and nurture your energetic vibration.

Worry and fear are some of the lowest vibrational states. When we are in these states, we are unknowingly attracting more of what we do not want. Knowing you have the power to choose your state of being (thoughts and emotions) and vibration (energy) is the first step to mastering your reality. Ultimately, learning how to stop the self-sabotage is the key. Learning how to discern what energy is yours versus that of others is also essential, as is learning how to shield yourself from lower energies and how to set energetic boundaries.

Have you ever been in a state where you feel extremely low or depleted but you don't understand why? It's not that you are down or anxious. In fact, maybe everything is going great in your world but you feel bad anyway. If that's the case, you're most likely in need of an energetic cleanup. You are walking around, carrying other people's stuff without knowing it.

As an empath, I have learned this over time through both my experiences and my children's experiences. When their dad died, for example, we would feel the grief the other was feeling. In fact, we were wrapped up in each other's grief. Without fail, when I had a bad day, my daughter would call to come home from school because she was feeling off but didn't know why. This became a turning point for me to understand the impact our energy has on each other and how important it is to maintain our energy hygiene.

When our energetic field is open and clear, we manifest with ease and we feel elevated. When it is blocked, it is like we are walking around in a dusty cloud. Energy healing (like reiki) can help with restoring our field, but there are also steps we can commit to on a daily basis to empower ourselves and stay energetically clear. We will explore how to do this in Chapter 7.

The bottom line here is that learning how to stay consistently grounded in a high vibration is the trick to experiencing flow and ease in your life. This may sound very woo-woo, but it can be practical in helping you achieve the results and peace you want in your life.

And there is no better time than now for all of us to learn how to stay in a high energetic vibration. The pandemic has created so much fear and division in our lives that we are in a collective swirl of low vibrational states. In order to rise above this, we need to do our individual work on a continuous basis so that we can contribute to the collective consciousness of the planet and help create an elevated world – together.

Will you join me?

3
ELEVATED DEFINED

"I'm the king of the world!"
"I'm flying, Jack!"
—Titanic

"OMG, I feel so great. I am unstoppable! I can do anything! Now ... how do I stay here?"

THIS is what I hear so often from my clients after we complete our work together (or at least the hard stuff), and it is exactly why I wrote this book. While it may feel like the major task in life is to overcome grief, find a dream job or manifest a soulmate, once we achieve any of those things, we aren't just done. Yes, we may feel like the king or queen of the world, but the moment is fleeting. We are never done growing, learning or living. (Well, unless you are done with your lifetime on earth, and even then you aren't really done either – but that's covered in my next book!)

Here's the thing, to stay in the flow of an elevated state, you must do your work every day – moment by moment. It is in these moments when we choose to be in a high vibration or not. It is our power of choice that dictates our experience, and it is our recovery when we fall from grace that enables us to continue to grow, master and live in an even more elevated existence.

What do I mean by "an even more elevated existence"? It is when you feel in flow and everything just seems to be going your way, going right – bliss. Your work, your life, your relationships are just flowing, synchronicities like chance meetings are happening with ease and opportunities abound. It's like your antenna is tuned into good fortune, joy, love and peace. And, in many ways, that is exactly what is happening.

But it's also deeper, and it ties back to the work I mentioned earlier by David Hawkins. Hawkins, M.D, Ph.D., was a nationally renowned psychiatrist, physician, researcher, spiritual teacher and lecturer and author of many books, including "Power vs. Force." What I love about his work is that it is completely scientific and pragmatic. His life-changing work on consciousness found me at exactly the right moment. I stumbled upon it when I was looking for science to help explain how manifesting works. The fact that Hawkins passed away on the same day as Sean felt like a sign for me to dig deeper.

I threw myself into Hawkins' work, especially his Map of Consciousness. I embraced his teachings as a way of living, and have come to believe that he unlocked some holy grail with regard to staying in an elevated state.

I will explain this work in the simplest of terms because the application is more important for me to convey to you than the intricacies of the scientific work itself. Hawkins identified that our emotional state of consciousness emits a vibrational frequency. This level of frequency increases logarithmically with our emotional state. Hawkins was able to isolate specific emotional states on a continuum, and separate low vibrational states from higher vibrational states. The transcendent point between a low vibrational state to a high vibrational state is found at the emotion of courage. Courage is where we recognize we have the power to choose our emotional state. I found this fascinating because, as a coach, this is of course what I teach. Our power of choice is what gives us the freedom to live life on our terms. This is mindfulness, which leads us on an upward spiral toward the ultimate state of spiritual enlightenment.

The interesting thing is that the lower vibrations are where Hawkins discovered the majority of people (85%) reside. Fortunately, because a high vibration emits an exponentially higher vibration than a lower one, less of the population is needed to be above the line (above courage) to have an impact on the planet. However, the more we can all work to raise our vibration consciously, the more it will serve everyone. As a collective consciousness, we all feel the dominant vibration of the planet, and it can affect our baseline energy.

This is why raising our vibration is so important. It really isn't just a "woo-woo" thing but a determinant of our individual and collective experience. The further we ascend into a higher state of being, the more aligned we are with our true desires and our purpose.

From a higher vibrational state, you will attract more of what you want and less of what you don't. Even more importantly, you will allow in what is truly meant for your spiritual growth and path. You will always attract what is a vibrational match for you, which in essence defines the law of attraction (e.g., like attracts like).

In the following chapters, I will explain how you can uplevel your experience by applying the Map of Consciousness to your life to attain a higher state of existence. Of course, just knowing the elevated states of consciousness is not enough to get us there. We are human after all, and maintaining an elevated state takes discipline, discernment and practice just like going to the gym for your physical fitness or eating well to maintain your weight or immunity. Your emotional and spiritual well-being is no different. What will help you stay in your practice is the benefit of a higher state of well-being, and the actualization of abundance in the areas of life that you desire.

The process to help you ascend the stages of consciousness is what I have somewhat playfully coined as KARMA. Hawkins used to joke that the reason we want to learn the Map of Consciousness is because we want to fix our karma before we experience it. I heard this after I had developed my five-step KARMA process and thought it was fitting – again, another sign. These are the steps I will share in detail with you as you move through the book.

The first step in the KARMA process is K: knowing yourself. As with any personal development process, knowing yourself inside and out, having self-awareness and acknowledging your higher self is key. Without this step, you cannot be truly mindful or conscious. Once you have this level of connection with yourself, with your light and shadow side, you can make better choices to help you move forward and upward.

21

This leads us to the next step, A: aligned action. Ascending the levels of consciousness assumes that you are acting in alignment with what you want. In order to attain what you want, you must align your thoughts, emotions and actions with this state of being. Regardless of what you want in your life, you must be it to receive it. And the greater your alignment with your higher self, the more easily and quickly whatever it is you want will flow to you. True alignment goes beyond the outward appearances and external influences of ego and sets us up on a heart-centered and soulful path of true authenticity.

Once we are living into our authentic selves, we become painfully aware of how easy it is to fall out of alignment sometimes. It is through R, or raising our consciousness level, that we are able to elevate and sustain ourselves in this desired state. This is our daily work, and we will explore how to maintain a discipline that allows you to continue your growth and evolution.

The truth is, no matter how enlightened you are, you will get triggered. We all do! What matters, though, is how you respond and how quickly you recover. M, or managing your energy and vibrational frequency, is essential for you to help yourself be at your best and attain the life you desire and deserve. We must all accept our humanity here and have compassion for ourselves. The quicker you realize your slip, the faster you can get back in alignment. I will share some powerful reframes, mind-hacks and energy-shifting techniques to help you quickly get back to your center.

What you may notice is that no matter how much work you do on evolving to the next level, there is something in the way of you getting to where you ultimately want to be. It may feel like there is a ceiling you keep hitting in your ability to get whatever it is you are wanting. This is an abundance block. We all have an unconscious receiving level. To get where you truly desire to be, you need to discover your receiving level and receiving limit, which you unconsciously ascribe to yourself. I will share some common blocks that keep you from A, actualizing your abundance, and how to move past them to help you elevate beyond where you ever dreamed possible. You will have tools to move past self-sabotage for good.

Here we go!

4

KNOWING YOURSELF – THE GOOD, THE BAD, THE UGLY AND THE MAGNIFICENT

"Wherever you go, there you are."

—Thomas à Kempis

I t all starts with you. It is so easy to say when you get a new job, a new partner, a promotion or a new house that everything will work out for you. You will be finally happy or satisfied with your life. Perhaps, when you picture yourself in your dream scenario of choice, everything does in fact seem perfect. But what happens when that moment passes? What happens when you get a leak in that new home or you have a fight with a new romantic partner? Will your happy ending be enough? Or is it just the next step on an endless string of desires that distract you from true happiness?

Here's the thing: You will not be able to sustain any bliss or even satisfaction if you have not done the necessary work within. This is exactly why some people who win the lottery end up blowing through their jackpot and land right back where they started. Money, like anything else, is just energy. It makes you more of who you already are. No matter what you do, invest in or create, the outcome hinges on you.

Everyone has that girlfriend who says, "I keep attracting the same guy." The guys may look different or work in different industries, but underneath it's always the same thing. Your friend is convinced this all points to an indisputable fact: There are no good men out there.

Do you ever scratch your head, and say to yourself, "I love you but, honey, maybe it's you?" Bingo. Yes, it's her. Yes, it's you. Yes, it's me. Everything we attract into our life, the good, the bad, the ugly and the magnificent, is because of us. We put out a signal of what we feel, believe, deserve and unconsciously want every second. That dominant vibrational frequency is powerful, and we receive what matches it. Given this, the best thing you could do for yourself in any scenario, especially in relationships, is work on you. While you can fake your mood or how you show up around others, you can't fake your vibration. It just is.

That's why investing your time in working on your mindset, beliefs, behaviors and energy is so critical. That's how you can start shifting your reality.

This starts with knowing yourself intimately – all parts, your shadow side and your light. In my first book, "Know What You Want Next," I go deep on how to do this by introducing the concept of your Inner Medusa. You Inner Medusa is your ugly side. She is the one who stops you from receiving what you really want. In fact, she keeps you paralyzed exactly where you are out of fear and protection. She is born out of your old patterns of survival, and she tries to keep your inner child in a safe and familiar place. When your inner child gets triggered (by something someone says, fear of rejection, the feeling of not being good enough, etc.), your Inner Medusa swoops in to save the day and say STOP to anything that feels unfamiliar, even if it is good for you or helping you to uplevel.

Learning what triggers your inner child and awakens your Inner Medusa is essential to shifting your vibration. When you learn how to identify these repeating patterns, you can start to mindfully disrupt them and choose something more aligned with your higher, magnificent, divine self.

The first step then is knowing and naming these parts of you – your Inner Medusa and your inner child. Once you have this level of awareness, you can start to observe the interplay. Recognizing how you respond and interact in different situations is literally like creating an out-of-body experience for yourself that is both mind-blowing and humbling. You will start to see how you may have created situations in the past that you might have unfairly blamed on others.

I experienced this firsthand when I started to date my husband, Ron. My Inner Medusa, I call her Sharon, went to every length to keep me (my little Kimmy) from feeling abandoned. Whenever I would feel the trigger that perhaps he might leave me, Sharon would emerge as a badass bitch and practically push him away first in an attempt to protect me from being hurt. Thank goodness I was able to share this with Ron so that he could understand exactly what was happening while I mastered my Sharon.

The good news? When you are in sync with the workings of your inner child, you will notice just how powerful you are in creating your own reality. You will also see how your inner child has been running the show for longer than you might've thought. This will likely motivate you to change. And if you have a patient partner like mine, you can ask them to help you by spotting your patterns before they derail you.

Opening your eyes to this inner dynamic will be the catalyst for transformation. Most likely if you are reading this book, you are already aware and working on this to some extent. This is what personal development and mastery of self is all about. Knowing your true self (the good), knowing your triggers (the bad), knowing your shadow (the Inner Medusa) and acknowledging that there is a magnificent inner goddess or higher self that exists within you all sets the stage for change. You are at choice at every moment to decide who sits at the head of the table and calls the shots.

BEYOND BADASS

You may recognize other parts of you, too. Vestiges of your past selves can emerge, like the rebel teenager or the take-no-prisoners executive. These personas may have protected or helped you in other areas of your life. No matter who appears, understand that all of these "people" or personas have a role in your life and play a part in your past, present or future.

Sometimes the persona is not one from your past so much as one you've chosen to put on in the present. I have a client who talks about her former "sledgehammer self" – her "badass" side. The one who climbed the corporate ladder to become one of two women in a major financial firm. She had to show badass to get where she is today. But the next level of living requires a different way of being. What she really wants now is to be her true self – to have strong boundaries but show up with more compassion and grace and ease in her life. This is how we ascend and flow.

I remember during my corporate days how I thought being intimidating was a plus. It made me feel powerful and strong and, quite honestly, safe to be wearing my designer clothes and sleek heels – my suit of armor. I remember feeling protected as long as I had the right outfit. I also fit the part a bit. I was badass in the way I acted and treated others – being intimidating was a badge of power. It got me ahead for sure, but did I really like who I was? Not really. It wasn't until I reflected on my behavior much later in life that I saw just how ruthless I was at times. Being badass was like a way to hide my true self at work, hold it all together and keep it going.

I know it some ways it helped me to cover the shame or feelings of unworthiness or "not good enough-ness." So, in that sense, it was helpful: I could step into my courage of putting myself out there. But today, with the corporate world behind me, I no longer need or want this mask to hide behind. In fact, when I feel it activate in my body, like a trigger – my old badass self – I take a few deep breaths and assess if she is really needed right now. I get curious about why she is showing up at that moment. Do I really need to protect myself? Or is it an old pattern that I can shift?

My elevated version of my badass self is my nurturing self. She is wise, strong, discerning, graceful and compassionate. She was really born after Sean died. I remember having to be so strong that I felt like I was wearing armor around others, especially around the other mothers in town. The whispers and rumors when I would walk by was enough to knock me down for the day. Going to school pick-up was the hardest part of my day. I would literally get into my badass, Beyonce self to shield myself from the stares that felt like bullets.

Slowly, the armor started to fade away as I began to work on myself and I learned to forgive. I forgave my husband, myself and even those who made my life harder during that time. I realized that holding that anger and keeping it together was too much for me. Letting it all go and allowing myself to just be me, the me I wanted to be, was much more appealing and freeing. I softened into the idea of letting love and kindness and an open heart guide me. I found that it was from this perspective, beyond badass, where I was truly free. Living into a heart-centered and loving way of being brought me back to me – the real me. I didn't have to be tough or hide. I could just be authentically me.

And when I brought that version of me to others, I found connection, kindness and peace. It was also the gateway to my life shifting into ways I'd never envisioned before. Synchronicities, possibilities and opportunities are everywhere. When we drop the badass armor, we reveal our truth and step into flow.

CHOOSING YOUR HIGHER SELF

Who do you want running the show going forward? That is the question. Therapy or coaching can help you understand just how each of these players came to be a part of you, but now you get to mindfully choose what the rest of your life is gonna be like. Drifting into your Inner Medusa is like doing a free fall into a low vibration. It's a place you may need to go once in a while to vent or have a hissy fit, but it is not a place where you want to stay.

Imagine yourself when you get to these depths. Visualize yourself on a trampoline bouncing back. Let yourself go as high as you can when you come back. Visualize yourself as your higher goddess rising over the earth and ocean, swirling higher and higher like a mermaid or fairy would. Feel this in your body and soul; breathe into it. Remind yourself of who you truly are and who you truly want to be, and let that feeling guide you to a higher state.

When you are connected to your higher self, your world will feel different. You will notice that whatever is going on around you is not as important as how you are doing on the inside. This is powerful. This is what to focus on day after day.

In order to strengthen this connection with your higher self and to proactively work toward staying in an elevated state, I suggest bookending your days with a meditative ritual designed to keep you rooted in your higher self.

Every morning, journal your appreciation for your life as it is and how you wish it to be as if it were already so. Then declare who you are. Name who you are and who you are becoming in the present moment using the declarative statement "I AM." As simple as this seems, it is potent. When you ascribe ways of being to yourself in a positive, receptive and powerful way, you begin to believe it and ultimately become it.

Begin with "I am" statements that are already true and that you want to maintain or elevate. Then add in declarations of what you want to be or embody more of. This is in essence what you need to be in order to receive what you want and live the life you want. Your soul knows exactly what this definition is, so if you are stuck, go inward and receive the answers through meditation. Do some journaling or automatic writing, where you write seamlessly without lifting your pen until the answer flows through you. This is your divine connection with your higher self and source energy. You will receive what you need.

Once you have the "I am" statements (or what I call your manifesto – the definition of who you are becoming), you can put it to work. Choose four to five "I am" statements where you have the biggest gaps. That means, on a scale of one to 10, where you score lowest in terms of embodying that quality or way of being right now. Those are your gaps, and identifying them is a game changer that will connect you with your higher self and give you both a goal and roadmap for what to focus on.

I recommend that you revisit this list every six weeks or so. You will see that, by focusing your attention and intention on these qualities, you will indeed embody them more. Rescore yourself and notice how you have mastered these qualities of being. Once you have integrated them into your essence, you are ready for the next level of growth. This is the time to elevate your "I am" statements to that next level.

Below is an example of a client's lists. At the start of our work together, she wrote:

1. I am worthy.
2. I am good enough.
3. I deserve good things.
4. I am confident.
5. I am successful.

After six months of doing this work, her ELEVATED list looked like this:

1. I am a goddess!
2. I am a powerful creator in my life!
3. I am abundantly wealthy!
4. I am unstoppable!
5. I am a $1m entrepreneur!

I worked with another client for almost three years, and each year she elevated her state so much that her business expanded tremendously. She moved twice in the span of three years because she had outgrown each space. She even added a second location to her practice. She continues to expand and soon enough will have a bicoastal presence in her business.

You will see your own growth and embodiment in your revised lists. You will feel a shift in enthusiasm and belief in yourself when you see the difference between your two lists.

Creating the manifesto and affirming who you want to be is the first step, but that alone is not enough. You must take action too. In the next chapter, we will discuss how to put this declaration into practice so you can stay aligned with your higher self and continue to receive and grow at that level.

5
ALIGNED ACTION

"You must be it to receive it."

—Unknown

Aligned action. This is the real secret that is often left out of law-of-attraction teaching. Yes, thoughts and visualizations matter for manifesting, but the most important step is action. We cannot just think ourselves rich, successful, happy, empowered, loved and courageous. We have to act in alignment with what we desire.

Because the universe is always responding to the frequency of our vibration, we cannot fake it. But at the same time, we have to start somewhere. Let's say, for example, you desire a soulmate relationship – a relationship with someone who shows you unconditional love and respect. Well, you will only be able to attract this if you are vibrating on the frequency of unconditional love and respect. This means that all of your wishes and visualizations are for naught if you cannot actually become what you desire yourself. This is aligned action.

This looks like you providing towards yourself the unconditional love and respect that you desire. You offer first this way of being in the world. This is the quickest way for it to manifest. Now, your actions must come from an authentic place, or your frequency will not be a vibrational match to what you want. THAT is the secret sauce right there. However, if you are not really feeling this vibration, start by acting as if you are. Ultimately, the more you practice with intention, the more you will start to embody this. Once it is embodied, you will receive.

Stepping into aligned action again requires you to do your inner work because it truly is the only way to attract what you want. Becoming a vibrational match to your desired outcome is an ongoing practice – you have to embody that state. As you do this work, you will notice that your focus changes. You'll become less and less attached to what you want and more and more resonant with the feeling that you desire. You'll start to see that the way you feel in a given state is more important than whatever you're trying to manifest. And, ironically, that is usually the point when all that you have ever wanted rushes right to you.

I remember when I was ready for a relationship again after my husband died. I really wanted to be with someone who had been through some form of loss similar to mine, had done the work to heal and could still choose to see each day as magnificent and beautiful. I wanted someone who had an appreciation for life and its little joys. I was also always very clear that I wanted him to really like and respect who I was, and show appreciation for me in little ways. Not surprisingly, these were things lacking in my marriage before. In order to manifest this, I realized that I needed to start treating myself the way I wanted someone else to treat me. This meant I had to like and respect myself. I had to show appreciation for myself in little ways. It wasn't just something I could tell myself in a mantra every day. I had to act as if this were true and start to believe it for myself through my own actions.

That is exactly what I did. I started to talk differently to myself. I started to have more compassion and respect for who I was. I actually slowed down enough to appreciate things throughout my day. I bought myself little gifts, like flowers to show myself I deserved those. I even bought myself a ruby ring as a token of my love for who I was becoming. I deserved nice things. I told myself I was worthy. I would take myself out on dates to a nice dinner and a movie. I did not wait for someone to take me; I did these things for myself.

I also worked on becoming more unconditional in my love towards others. I started to live into this vibration of love and appreciation of those around me, and my world started shifting. I noticed how people around me were more giving and appreciative of me. I could feel the difference within me and around me, and others could too. And ultimately, I did manifest a soulmate who I honestly can say loves me unconditionally and shows his appreciation for me every day.

As I was mindfully choosing on a daily basis to be in an elevated state of love and appreciation, I noticed that all sorts of beautiful things were coming my way – even things I had longed for before that I no longer desired. This is the funny thing about aligned action. This is when the old high school boyfriend often resurfaces in your life. Aligned? Probably not … maybe … definitely check in with yourself.

When you are in alignment with your higher self, manifestations happen quickly and often effortlessly.

However, you must know that just because something comes to you, it does not mean it is for you. You must be discerning. This, I often say, is the test of the Universe. When you are in a high vibration connected to your higher self, you are shiny and bright and so many things are attracted to your light. You must dig deep and get grounded in your core and trust your intuitive sense if something is right or wrong for you. I always have to remind myself that not everything is a sign. The question is, is it aligned with you now?

Checking in with your body to see if this is aligned with you and where you are now is key. And if it is not, you must let it go. That is the test. If you do follow through on honoring yourself with aligned choices, you will notice that you are rewarded quickly for doing so. If you don't, you will notice you get more of the same. The pattern will repeat until you disrupt it and choose something different – choose to *be* different. By acquiescing, it is as if you are saying to the Universe, "Yes, please send me more of this."

So how do you know for sure if something is aligned with you or not? Your body never lies. You can do a simple scan of your body and notice, when you think of something, how your body feels. If it is right for you – aligned with your truth, a YES – then you will feel a lightness and ease in your belly and maybe some excitement and expansiveness in your heart center. If it is a no, you will feel it in your gut or your chest, or maybe even your head. It could feel like a pit in your stomach, a feeling of dread in your gut. Or maybe your chest feels tight and you feel a lump in your throat. If you are having a hard time discerning at first, start with things you already know the answers to and do a body scan going forward with your decisions. You will start to trust yourself to get the answer you seek.

If you are still struggling with indecision, there are other ways you can get the answers you seek. Muscle testing, for example, is a way to objectively observe yourself and your decisions. Stand up and put your right hand about a foot over your head. Now, ask yourself a yes/no question. Notice how your body moves. If it is true or a yes, you will move forward. If it is false or a no, then your body will move backward. You can start with something as simple as your name. This is a way to be sure your system is in alignment from the start. Then continue to ask other questions. Is this job right for me? Is Rick a good fit for me? Should I continue working with Susan? Should I stay in Florida? The answers really should not surprise you, and will start helping you to trust your intuition.

You are simply reading your own energy here. You can also do this with an instrument like a pendulum.

Aligned Action

Pendulums are a fun way to get a quick answer on alignment. You can make a pendulum with just a piece of string and a paper clip if you don't have a proper one. Simply hold the pendulum over your hand, and ask that it show you "yes." Notice which way the pendulum swings – often vertically. Then ask that it show you "no." You will notice the pendulum switch directions to go horizontal. Ask another question, and you will see how easily the pendulum picks up on your energy. Now, the only caveat is that you can't really ask predictive questions like, "Does Joe like me?" Or, "Will I get the promotion?" You can have fun with that for sure, but the pendulum is really just picking up on your energy and your vibration, so you will get validation of what you already think. The pendulum is essentially a tool to help you see the truth of what you already believe.

Lastly, as you start to ascend into your higher self, it is important to stay in alignment with the values of who you are and who you are becoming. You may notice how easily you manifest some latent desires, as I mentioned earlier. While these things may have been something you wanted a short time ago, they may not fit who you are now. In addition to checking in with your body, check in with your soul. Ask yourself if something serves your soul or your ego. Is it moving you further along into ascension or pulling you back into fulfilling your ego or feeding your fears – fear of missing out or an egotistical desire for being seen, for instance.

Remember you are always at choice. This is where you get to choose powerfully the path forward – to be in an elevated state or not. Be discerning.

6
RAISING YOUR CONSCIOUSNESS

"The decision to overlook the seeming inequities of life instead of reacting to them is a choice."
—David Hawkins

'm sure you've heard the expression, "Life is happening for you, not to you." It took me a long time to fully understand the meaning of these words. Surely life is happening around me and there are things I cannot control. I did not choose for my husband to take his life, for example, nor could I control the pandemic. These are external forces that have nothing to do with my actions.

While I cannot orchestrate the world around me, I can control how I react to things and how I choose to experience them. I can choose to come from a place of love, grace and understanding, or from a place of anger, resentment and fear. While one may sometimes require more work on my part, it is still my choice.

Being free to make this choice is your spiritual right. And when you make choices aligned with your higher self and the betterment of the world, your reality changes. You have probably felt this internal shift before. It feels so good to live within your truth and authentic self. That alone can sometimes propel you to continue making aligned choices and be your best self. However, as humans, it is normal to slip in and out of being our best selves in response to life's challenges and rewards. And we are never immune to the unconscious triggers that can impede our ability to show up as our best. Recognizing when it happens and recovering quickly with self-compassion is the key.

Choosing to live more consciously day to day is a significant commitment to ourselves, our livelihood, our families and our society. It takes a lot of strength, resilience, courage and love to bring our best even when the chips are down and life feels hard. I mentioned before how easy it is for me to fall down the shame well when I get triggered. When feelings of "not enough-ness" crop up, I can easily find even more reasons to feed that narrative. Choosing to shift in that moment to a higher vibration – one of love and gratitude – can be easier sometimes more than others.

But there's another reason why it is essential for you to make this shift as quickly as possible, and it's one that benefits everyone around you. This is the game changer you have been looking for to keep you grounded in your higher self.

When I stumbled upon David Hawkins' research on the Maps of Consciousness, I was looking for scientific evidence to support the law of attraction and manifesting. In his work, I found that and more. His work has uncovered some keys to the magical workings of the Universe and can be a roadmap for the rest of us in creating a world where joy and peace can reign.

THE LEVELS OF CONSCIOUSNESS

David Hawkins stated, "To become more conscious is the greatest gift anyone can give to the world; moreover, in a ripple effect, the gift comes back to its source." When we talk about consciousness, it can sound so lofty and out of reach, like some nebulous thing in the universe. But consciousness is quite simply a state of being. When you choose your state of being, you are conscious. Your world will also be more aligned with a higher state of consciousness and fit in more seamlessly with the collective consciousness – meaning you will feel at one with all things. Our consciousness as a collective is more important than we often think, and our individual impact on the collective is more potent than many believe.

When considering your life today, how conscious is your living? Are you living on autopilot? Are you stuck in the rat race of daily life? Or are you living life consciously on your terms? This is the first step for raising your level of consciousness.

For me, I spent the better part of my life in the depths of unconscious living until I woke up after Sean's suicide. Oftentimes, life has to send a wake-up call to get us on the spiritual path of healing and conscious living.

But what if you could just start doing that now without any big disruption to your life? What if you could just ascend to a higher state of living from where you are this moment? Maybe you think, "Well, my life is pretty good the way it is, so why mess with it?" Let me show you why.

DIAGRAM OF MAP OF CONSCIOUSNESS
BY DAVID HAWKINS

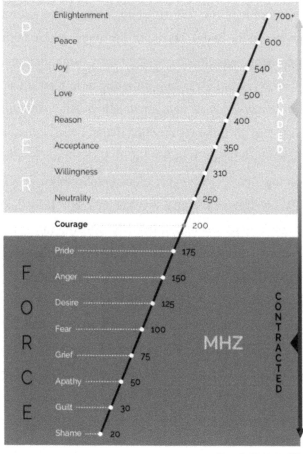

POWER VERSUS FORCE:
MAP OF CONSCIOUSNESS

Enlightenment		700+
Peace		600
Joy		540
Love		500
Reason		400
Acceptance		350
Willingness		310
Neutrality		250
Courage		200
Pride		175
Anger		150
Desire		125
Fear		100
Grief		75
Apathy		50
Guilt		30
Shame		20

Source: David R. Hawkins, PhD

Elevated

Hawkins was able to determine the vibrational energetic state associated with every emotion. From this, he was able to distinguish emotional states that are considered low vibrational or false (meaning they create a weak response in the body) from those that are high vibrational or true (meaning they create a strong response in the body). He did this through muscle testing experiments over the course of 20 years using millions of calibrations from a random sampling of human subjects (representative of all ages, nationalities and emotional well-being) in different emotional states and situations. His work satisfies the test of the scientific method, meaning it has perfect experimental replicability.

What Hawkins found was the energetic field (a.k.a. the aura) increased logarithmically with the increase in the emotional state. For instance, he found the lowest-level emotion to be shame in which the energy field vibrated at only 20 MHz. The greatest emotional state of enlightenment had a vibration of 1,000 MHz. He found the transcendent point from a lower state to a higher state of consciousness occurred at the emotional state of courage (200 MHz). This is when we believe we are at choice and feel empowered in our life; we do not see ourselves as victims. We feel a sense of freedom and personal power, and it is reflected in our energy.

Remember that anecdote I shared in Chapter 4 about putting on a badass persona to climb the corporate ladder? It applies here, too. Women have embraced this term as a positive concept for a long time, and probably because it can help get you from fear to pride to courage. The drawback? It comes with some baggage.

The definition of badass is an intimidating person. This is not necessarily how you attract what you want, but simply deflect what you don't want. To be open to receiving and leveling up your state of consciousness, you need to relax into a more heart-centered, open way of being. You need to take off your badass armor and reveal your vulnerable self and truth. *That* is how you elevate and connect with others.

I really see "badass" as a defensive word rather than an empowering one. In fact, I see it as an unhelpful way of being if you want to get to a state of elevated consciousness. When we can let go of that narrative and allow ourselves to melt into our feminine energy, we are even more powerful and inviting. We can co-create at our highest levels and raise the vibration around us. When we move beyond badass and vibrate higher, we achieve grace.

It's no wonder women have resorted to the badass persona to achieve courage. Hawkins found that only 15% of the population vibrates above courage. The majority is stuck in a dominant vibration below the line of courage. In other words, the majority of our planet is living unconsciously – a false truth. The research suggests to me that our goal in this lifetime should be to learn how to vibrate above the line – to live consciously. To navigate the depths of lower vibrations and consciously choose to ascend them.

This is not to say you should not feel grief or shame at times, but we should not park there. This work is truly a gift and gives us permission to say, "Enough!" to our guilt, shame, fear and pride. These emotions are toxic to the system. While there may have been years of programming and societal conditioning to promote these emotions within us, Hawkins' scientific findings serve as our permission slip to let it all go! Process, shift and move on.

Interestingly enough, there is a pathway to move from one emotional state to another. While shame (or inward hate) is the lowest of the low, guilt, blame, apathy and fear (outward hate) vibrate a little higher. But anger is a catalyst that helps you move past these lower vibrational states. Once ascending anger, you start to resonate with some self-esteem, although it's still false at pride/ego/ desire. The states of pride and desire are higher because they are at least in line with caring for oneself, but they are coming from a place of self-centeredness that emits a lower vibration of greed and lack of compassion towards others. Pride and ego are where Hawkins identified the majority of humans residing in their dominant vibration.

Not surprisingly, you can see why some life event is often required to break this state of self-absorption. Something usually has to wake us up from this sleepy state so we can see beyond ourselves and gain some empathy. Once we wake up to the facts that we are part of something bigger, that we have some agency and influence over our lives and that we can be victors in our lives and not just victims of circumstance, we become empowered and enter the stage of courage.

HIGHER CONSCIOUSNESS

With only 15% of us residing above the line of courage most of the time, you can see how it can really be lonely at the top. Reaching this higher level of consciousness is no joke. It takes discipline and a belief in something bigger than the material plane. Once we reach the elevation of courage, we can see more than we've ever seen before. It's like we've unlocked a world and freedom that others just don't know about. It takes daily work to stay in this vibration and even more to ascend it.

To get beyond courage, I believe it's necessary to do a life-inventory assessment. We must really look in the mirror and say, "OK, what do I need to fix, amend and correct to ascend?" For me, I felt this enormous shift within myself after my husband died. I had to get to a place of radical acceptance of what had happened while not ever fully understanding why it happened. I ultimately had to embrace all that had happened from a place of forgiveness and love. This was not easy, but the shame was too huge to carry around with me. Hawkins refers to shame as "passive suicide." I could feel that happening to me day by day, and I needed to decide to choose something different for me and for my girls. I knew in those moments that what I had to model for them was how to live. I decided that joy would be better. From that day forward, I began to live from a place of joy – what Hawkins calls unconditional kindness – and my life dramatically shifted.

Now I did not have this Map when I was going through my wake-up call. I only found it years later, but let me tell you I am living proof that it works. When I began to live from a place of unconditional love, joy, kindness and forgiveness, my world became completely different. What was different was really how I experienced my life, the people who came into it and the opportunities and beauty that were suddenly open to me. Even with all I had been through, life flowed effortlessly and miracles manifested without much effort or prayer. The Universe was supporting me as if on command.

This was very affirming for me because when you are grieving and you finally decide you are done with that, not everyone is ready for your decision. When I was ready to move forward into love, I encountered many harsh judgments and criticisms: that it was too soon, or I was not ready to make that decision so fast. People's expectations were not aligned with where I was living. They could not see what I could see and feel. I was magnetically attracting a vibrational match of love and joy into my life so fast that it did not make sense to others. I know this is because I allowed myself to choose joy over grief. To choose love over fear. To choose acceptance and forgiveness over anger and blame. When you allow yourself to rise into a higher vibrational emotional state, your reality shifts to match that frequency. That alone is reason enough to give yourself the gift of higher consciousness.

But there is more. When you elevate your state, it raises the consciousness around you. Because everything is energy and because we are all connected as energy, your vibration affects others and vice versa. So, if you can allow yourself to consciously continue to raise your state, you will help those around you. And imagine if they do their work too! What a world it would be.

This is why everyone could feel the energy around them during the pandemic. We were swimming in so much fear, and collectively weighed down by shame and blame, that I imagine the vibrational frequency on the planet was lower than average during that time. To combat this, meditation and prayer are powerful tools. Joy vibrates more than 10 times higher than fear, so it does not take as many people to be emitting joy to start to cancel out the planetary vibration of fear. This is why group meditation, prayer and song are so powerful for healing. While we cannot visibly see their effects, they do have a profound and palpable impact.

The Hawaiian Forgiveness Prayer, *Ho'oponopono*, even has scientific backing for its collective healing effects. These four simple but powerful lines used in meditation, "*I love you, I am sorry, Please forgive me, Thank you,*" are credited with helping reform prisoners and restoring peace to villages. I can also speak to the impact that these words had on my own healing after the death of my husband. I would recite these lines every morning to release the guilt and shame I felt regarding Sean's suicide. These words feel like a cleanse across your whole system, and they allow you to let go of any pain and suffering you are holding onto. It is a visceral release that brings peace.

Hawkins said, "Love is misunderstood to be an emotion; actually, it is a state of awareness, a way of being in the world, a way of seeing oneself and others." Love is the antidote to fear and lower vibrations. When we ascend to love, which is unconditional, we live differently. We see the world as a benign place. It's easier for us to see the silver linings and have compassion for ourselves and others. We are open to giving and receiving without expectation or conditions.

This is a place where not many are able to reside. Less than 10% of people achieve this level of consciousness in their lifetime. This does not mean they will not experience love or find love, but they won't reside within the state of being that is love. They won't show up, heart-centered, in their everyday and maintain a love-based outlook on life and all things.

To get to this state of love, you must learn to let go of your burdens and your attachments to desires, and allow yourself to follow your heart and spirit for guidance. It is at this point when you start to realize that you are not just an individual but part of a greater collective consciousness. You start to build your connection to divinity. As you move up from love to joy to peace to enlightenment, your level of unconditional compassion and connection to the divine grows exponentially. Only a few make it to this level of enlightenment, like the great spiritual teachers Jesus, Krishna and Buddha.

I'll take the leap of faith in you to add this: I do believe that governments try to separate people from their beliefs and sever their connection to the divine because it ultimately enhances their control and power. I don't say this from one political party or fringe group with an agenda, but as an individual who recognizes her place in the collective: It is interesting how politicians, the media and advertisers strive to keep us in the depths of the low vibrations of fear, shame and blame. Being in a lower vibration keeps someone stuck in a victim mentality, which makes that person easier to control. Our best defense is to work on our spiritual ascension and inspire others to do the same.

Raising Your Consciousnesss

Now that we have more ammunition for why we want to be in this place of elevation, let's work on getting there consciously.

7
MANAGING YOUR ENERGY

"Good vibes only."

—Everyone

I t seems like you hear people talking about "good vibes" just about everywhere these days. It is a Californian cliché for sure, but deep below the surface there is good stuff there. When we talk about maintaining good vibes, we are really speaking of managing our energetic frequency. Despite the fact that our energy field is predictive of our experience in life, we usually don't tune into it. Or, worse, we straight-up ignore it. Neither pathway is very beneficial.

The body never lies, and neither does our energy. When someone walks into the room, you can feel their energetic impact. More than what they say or do, it's their energy that elicits a response, it's their energy that you remember.

That's the explanation behind meeting someone at a party and connecting immediately (or not!). There are some people you could talk to all night, and there are others you, well, just want to avoid. That's energy – and you can't hide it.

You can, however, work on raising your vibrational state and thus the energetic frequency you emit. As Hawkins proved in his research, the higher the emotional state, the higher the energetic vibrational state. So, it's no wonder you feel safer sharing with someone who is in a higher energetic and emotional state of love and joy than someone who is fearful and ego-based. You don't have to ask them how they are feeling to know; you can sense the energy they give off.

I have intuitively understood this from an early age; you probably have too. I remember having an uncanny ability as a child to distinguish someone who was honest and true from someone who was jealous and fake. It served me well as an adult because I knew who to avoid, but when I was younger, it often got me into messes. I would be chastised by my friends for being judgmental even though most of the time my assessment turned out to be right. I began to keep my thoughts to myself more, which was probably a good idea anyway, and now I just watch things play out. I know instantly who is a fit for my energy and who is not. This can make for some lonely nights, but in the end, I feel safer and happier. Ultimately, this has helped me to cultivate a better relationship with myself and learn to enjoy my own company more.

When we feel this energetic impact from others, it is important to note that we can sometimes pick up on more than we bargain for. I am sure you have heard the term "energy vampires," and I bet you have experienced them too. These are the folks who leave you feeling 100% depleted after you spend any time around them. Hawkins pointed out these are often people in a low vibration, and being around them for too long will indeed drain you. Protecting yourself and setting energetic boundaries is essential for maintaining your high vibration. And quite honestly, as you work on ascending the levels of consciousness, these people will start to shift out of your life. In the beginning, this may feel hard. You may not get invited to the same parties or events, and you will not be top of mind with them. Remind yourself that is OK. You are instead open to new people and experiences that are a vibrational match for where you are at the moment and where you are going next.

If we could all see energy the way many clairvoyants can, it would make life a lot easier. You would know on sight who to avoid. But the truth is you need to take care of your energetic body just like you do your physical one. There are many things that can lower your vibration on both a physical and an energetic level. Knowing and respecting these influences are essential to keeping you on your ascension path. And just like going to the gym, energy work is a daily commitment. You will feel it if you miss a day. You will feel like you got slimed – exhausted and icky – even if you don't know why. That means it's time to clean up your energetic field and shield it going forward.

Getting depleted can happen other ways, too. Sometimes, we give away too much of our energy. Other times, someone is cording into us and draining our energy. What do I mean by cording? When we interact with others, we can form energetic cords with them through our words, thoughts and emotions. These cords connect our energy fields, which allows energy to flow between us.

If someone has energetically corded into your field, you may feel exhausted, like you are running on empty.

I'll talk more about cords in a minute, but let's first look at how we can get depleted and neglect our own needs. I recently had a client tell me that she wakes up every morning thinking about whether or not she is OK in her relationships. She is always worried someone might be upset with her. This external worry keeps her unnecessarily trapped in a low vibration.

I lived like this for years in my first marriage – walking on eggshells and disconnected from myself. If you are stuck in this place now, start shifting your focus to your internal self. Start deliberately allowing yourself to make your joy your focus. When you wake up in the morning, jump out of bed and do a victory pose and say, "I am grateful for this day. I am grateful to be alive. I am grateful to be me!" I did this for months when I really did not feel it, but eventually I started to believe in the gratitude and looked forward to each day.

When our energy is depleted for a very long time, it can actually start to make us physically ill, so it's really important that you take care of your energy body before it affects your physical body. If you find yourself going into fear, blame or shame, then it's time to clean up your energy and raise your vibration.

YOUR ENERGY BODY

What is your energy body, you ask? Your energy body is your energy field or aura. There are many layers to the aura, but I am going to focus on the basics here.

Your energetic body is like an invisible blueprint around your physical body, and it is fueled by seven energy centers called *chakras* (which means "wheel" in Sanskrit). I am sure you have some level of awareness of this. I was late in my discovery, and it was not until my 40s that I found reiki energy healing and became certified in it. Reiki is a Japanese form of energy healing that uses spiritually guided life-force energy to release stress and provide healing. The word "reiki" comes from the Japanese word *rei*, which means "universal life" and *ki*, which means "energy."

I should say that reiki really found me. It happened a couple of months after Sean had died and I found myself at an event at our town library. There, I won a raffle for a reiki treatment – in a raffle that I had never entered! I didn't know what to expect at my first session, but I was open to receive whatever it brought me. My reiki master, Cecile, tuned into the pain of loss, broken heart and fear that were within me. She told me in that session that she had repaired my heart chakra and that I would find love again if I could keep my heart center open.

Early in my spiritual awakening, I was also drawn to the work of Barbara Brennan. Brennan was a scientist for NASA, is a renowned energy healer and teacher and is the author of "Hands of Light." Her name came to me in a meditation I was doing to help me identify my spiritual guide – Brennan. Another serendipitous connection happened about a year later when I met my now business partner and colleague, Katherine Glass. Katherine had trained with Barbara for years. It was clear to me from these connections that I was meant to learn the healing benefits derived from energy work. All of these workings together led me to decide to pursue energy healing training myself.

Some energy healers can see tears in the energy body. While I cannot see tears in the energy body, I have occasionally seen people's auras. I don't see the colors some people do, though: I only see them in black and white. After working with my clients through deep meditations and inner-child work, I have often seen a white glow around them, which indicates they are in a very positive state.

I have also seen the flipside. When someone is very sick, their energetic body may appear dark and gray. I had the most remarkable experience about six years ago. I was at a crowded event at my daughter's school. I was standing on a stairway looking down at a mass of people. My eyes were drawn to someone whom I knew fairly well. I had to do a double-take because when I saw him, it was as if he were inside a dark cloud. He literally had a dark shadow of light in and around him. It was like he was trapped in black-and-white, and everything that surrounded him was in vivid color. I said to myself but out loud, "He is going to die." I was in shock when I left the school that night. The next morning, I learned that he did indeed pass away that night.

We have many energy centers that keep our system flowing and in balance. There are seven major ones that we will focus on.

DIAGRAM OF SEVEN CHAKRAS

Seven Main Chakras

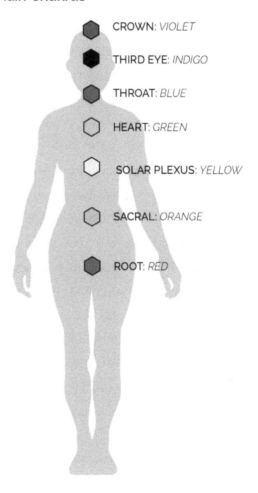

CROWN: *VIOLET*

THIRD EYE: *INDIGO*

THROAT: *BLUE*

HEART: *GREEN*

SOLAR PLEXUS: *YELLOW*

SACRAL: *ORANGE*

ROOT: *RED*

Chakras are arranged in the order of the rainbow, which makes it easy to remember: ROYGBIV. Each chakra controls a part of the body, which is connected with an emotion and state of being. I am going to briefly touch on these for demonstrative purposes to help you use this information in an actionable, pragmatic way. If you would like to go deeper – and I suggest you do – Brennan's work is a great place to start.

The first chakra, the root, is a juicy red color and is found at your tailbone. This chakra or energy wheel is connected with your security in the world: physical safety, finances, being grounded. When your root is off, you'll know it. You'll often feel untethered, ashamed and fearful.

Your second chakra is your sacral chakra, a bright orange, and it is connected to your sexual organs and source of creativity. If your libido is blocked, or if you feel a lack of creativity, you may be imbalanced here. Guilt or grief are other symptoms of a blocked sacral chakra.

Your third chakra is one that gets a lot of attention, and it is your solar plexus. Like a bright ball of yellow sunshine, this chakra is connected to your sense of power, and you want to be sure it is in balance and cleaned out regularly. People often cord into it (either consciously or unconsciously) and drain you.

Managing Your Energy

In our workshops, we do a lot of work to help people reclaim their power from others who have corded into them over time. These energetic cords are of course invisible, but you can feel it. To scan yourself for any cords, close your eyes and bring awareness to your solar plexus, which is right around the top of your ribcage below your chest. Notice if any person appears to your mind's eye. If they do, chances are they are cording into you. No one, not even your kids, should be corded into you (unless they are under 5). Now visualize pulling that cord out of your solar plexus and returning it to the person who appeared before you as you say, "I reclaim my power from you, and I release you."

You can perform this scan for any chakra, and I recommend you do it daily (sometimes more if you see clients on a regular basis).

Next is your heart chakra, which is in your heart center. This has a beautiful green energy or sometimes a watermelon pink energy. Focus on what feels right to you. You will want to release any energetic cords here too.

Often, when you are feeling hurt or betrayed, this chakra will be blocked, like mine was. To open your heart center, it is important to choose to forgive whoever has hurt you. This is also a way to help you shift your level of consciousness. While you cannot see the energy within your heart chakra, if you are holding onto resentment or anger towards another person, it blocks your heart center from fully receiving. If you want to receive love, you must choose to let go of the burdens that block you. In the early days of grieving my husband, I spent every morning consciously releasing the blocks around my heart by visualizing them opening and clearing as I forgave him and myself.

Your heart center is also where your electromagnetic field is the strongest. You need an open heart in order to receive love and anything that you want. To open your heart further, close your eyes during meditation, and imagine a beautiful pink light in your heart center. With each breath, imagine this pink light growing. As it grows, allow yourself to feel the sense of unconditional love that is within you expand. Imagine this light growing with each inhale and exhale so that it encompasses your whole body. Eventually, you will find yourself inside a beautiful ball of pink light. Now, allow yourself to dwell in this light and feel the love in and around you. Share this beautiful light out into the world. Know that you have this inside of you at all times and can share with yourself when you need it or with others when they need it. Return to your center, open your eyes and notice how you feel. You are now ready and open to receive. (You will also physically feel a shift in your energy field!)

Your throat chakra is a beautiful sky blue. When it is blocked, it is because we are refraining from speaking our truth. Do you find yourself constantly clearing your throat? If so, is there something that you are not sharing or speaking up about in your life? Keeping your throat chakra clear will keep you in alignment with your spoken truth. I once had a client who came to me with a rash all over her neck that she could not get rid of. She had tried everything. In our work together, we realized that she was holding back from speaking up in her relationships. Once she freed her voice, her rash cleared.

The last two centers are gateways to your higher consciousness. Your third-eye chakra resides between your brows and is an indigo color. This is where you experience your clairvoyance and invisible sight.

When you begin to meditate more regularly, you will often find that, when your eyes are closed, this beautiful shade of indigo fills the space. You can actually see it. This is a divine experience for sure. The first time this happened to me was during one of my reiki sessions with my reiki master, Cecile. It was like I could see my third eye open.

A burst of beautiful indigo light rushed through my brow center, and I started to see images I had never seen before. It felt a bit like I was hallucinating and floating. Visions of a white peacock drifted by me, and I even seemed to see Jesus and Mother Mary. I believe I was receiving images that were telling me I was safe and protected. Keeping your third eye clear will help you to connect with your intuition and trust yourself more.

Lastly, your crown chakra is where you connect with source energy. As you start to work on your energy centers, you will experience what it feels like when your crown opens to receive. (It feels like a tingling on the crown of your head.) This is where you receive divine guidance or messages from Spirit. As a medium, this is how I connect with loved ones in spirit, but this channel is open to everyone. When your crown and heart chakras are open and you are in a high state of consciousness (like love, joy or peace, for example) you are open to receiving signs from Spirit. Of course, you need to look for them and believe in them when you see them.

When we are in a low vibrational state like grief, our chakras are often blocked from receiving. This is why when a loved one dies, we do not always notice the signs from them right away. Once we start to heal and feel the spark of love and joy again, we can see the signs. Spirit consciousness vibrates at such a high frequency (I assume enlightenment) that we need to match the vibration to connect. This is obviously not easy to maintain. Meditation can help us get into this receiving mode. Psychics and mediums can help us connect more quickly because they are in tune with this frequency and have experience holding (or what's called linking) the energy and vibration longer.

The crown chakra is a beautiful violet color. You may even imagine it as pure white or gold. Pulling cords out of this chakra is important for maintaining your connection with source energy and Spirit. If you want to keep your connection with Spirit clean, you will want to disconnect any cords from outside sources that could compromise your clear reception, such as the news or societal beliefs that don't align with you. Just pull out the cords and release them.

As you release any energetic cords that are tugging on you, you will also want to fill your chakras with beautiful light and amplify them. You can do this by simply creating a ball of energy in your hands. (You have chakras in your hands, and you can feel the energy pulse between them.) Place a ball of light into each chakra that corresponds with its color and swirl it in. You can also just quickly go over each chakra and turn each one like you would a switch or dial. This may feel silly at first, but the more you do it, the more you will feel a sense of peacefulness and lightness. This is what it feels like to lift into a higher vibration.

Knowing that you are at risk of being "slimed" or corded, it is wise to protect your energy field. You can imagine yourself in a bubble or surrounded by a shield to protect your aura. If you know someone who does pull on your energy a lot, you will want to guard especially your solar plexus by not standing directly in front of the person or even physically covering this area of your body. Then, when you get home, cleanse your energy. (If you have ever felt this, you will know just how violating it can feel.)

I know some of this may sound extreme, but once you start to take care of your energy, you will see how things shift quickly. Also, you will feel healthier and get sick less often. A more precise way to do this is to regularly see a certified reiki master or energy healer. (And if you work with the public a lot, I recommend you have a weekly healing and continue to work on yourself daily.) After doing reiki daily on myself for seven years, I rarely get sick. I used to suffer from chronic sinusitis and annual bronchitis. I have not had a bout of either in years.

RAISING YOUR VIBRATION

In addition to working directly with your energy body, there are other conscious ways to raise your vibration. (This might take the form of healing from a low vibration or moving to an elevated state.) You can do this to impact your mind, body and spirit.

BODY

You can start with eating cleanly (more vegetables and less, if any, animal protein), exercising and practicing good hygiene. If you want to work on ascending to a higher level of consciousness, eating less and eating a more vegan diet will accelerate this. You may notice that when you do a cleanse, you feel clearer, lighter and more intuitive. This has been my experience anyway.

While it may be hard to implement this way of living, it is essential if you are serious about raising your vibration. Start with giving up processed foods, and then animal protein. Anything that is synthetic will clog your system. If you do eat an animal protein, be sure to clear the energy from the animal by blessing it before you eat it. This is why eating plants is a safer and more humane way of eating and living. (And it's more conducive to higher consciousness.) When you eat an animal, you are essentially taking on its energy and often the vibration of fear from when it was killed. I know this is awful to think about, but if everything is energy and energy transmutes rather than dies, you have to consider the source of what you are ingesting.

This may even spill over to the idea of who prepared you food. Making sure you know the source is essential to maintaining the vibration you want to embody. Have you ever felt strange after a meal out? I don't mean sick, but just off or somehow not right. My daughter experienced this recently where she felt odd after her meal and not like herself. She actually said that she felt like the chef was angry when he prepared her meal! She is very intuitive, and that possibly could have been the case. It is something to think about if you eat out often. Some religious sects even advise against having others prepare your meals for that very reason.

MIND

Feeding your mind is no different than feeding your body. You must adhere to positive, elevated thoughts and conversations. This means truly honoring a positive perspective of yourself and others – ditching judgment, gossip and sarcasm. Treating yourself and others from a place of unconditional love and kindness. You can see right there why it is so hard to sustain an elevated state or get to an enlightened state to begin with. This is moment-by-moment work to mind yourself and how you interact in the world. When you fall, and we all do, keep coming back to love and appreciation. Gratitude is a gateway to shift back into a higher state.

And pay attention to your words. They matter. Like emotions, every word has a vibrational state attached to it. Not surprisingly, words like love, peace and joy have a higher vibration than words like hate, destruction and the like. Feed yourself high vibrational words and use them in your everyday language. Resist the words that bring you down.

This includes song lyrics. Have you ever paid attention to what you listen to or sing along to? It does matter. Even my favorite band, U2, is not immune to this standard. Now, U2 is pretty harmless compared to some other contemporary music, but still, most of their music puts me in a weakened state when I look at the lyrics and tonality – sadness, fear, anger, desire, pride and maybe a hint of courage. It really does not get above the line much. Look into higher vibrational alternatives like Kundalini music or chanting to uplift you. Remember too that you are always manifesting, so words are working for you or against you in real time.

SPIRIT

Other ways to raise your vibration include daily meditation, prayer, sound healing and body movement like Kundalini Yoga. Be sure to keep your surroundings clean and clear from negativity and potential dark energy by burning sage or Palo Santo. And make sure that you open the windows and doors to let out the old energy. After your clear your surroundings, I like to infuse my space with positive energy using incense with lavender or essential oils and high vibrational music. I also do this at the start of every week. Before I write, I have a ritual where I infuse the space with high vibrational music, light candles and invite creativity.

Surrounding yourself with beauty and sacredness is an important way to elevate your space and shift the energy. After my husband passed, I cleared every room in the house several times to release any stagnant energy, and I infused each space with my own energy and preferences. We went from a beige house to a very vibrant and colorful home in a just a few months. This was very healing for me and a way to reclaim myself and set the stage for my next chapter. I do believe this helped me to manifest what was next for me. I was clearly showing myself and the Universe I was ready and worthy for something new and magical.

Stepping into nature is a way to instantly clear your energy, especially grounding, which is an ancient way of clearing. (Grounding means letting your bare feet connect with the earth as you allow yourself to just be in stillness.) Grounding lets your worries and fears melt away into the earth.

As you do this, open your arms and heart and crown to receive divine light. You will know just how you are vibrating when you are in nature by the way animals interact with you. Do they freeze or run past you? Or do they move slowly around you, perhaps even stare at or approach you, wanting to be in your presence? Many animals, especially domesticated ones, vibrate higher than we do. A dog's tail wag and a cat's purr, for example, vibrate at love at 500MHz. Yes, that is real, unconditional love you are feeling from them. And when you are in a high vibration, animals feel it too.

Ignite your joy by doing things that give you boosts of joy, like singing or dancing or whatever it is that does this for you. If you are not sure what those things are, make it your intention to find out. Elevate love and kindness in your life by putting more love and kindness in the world. When I was waking up from grieving, I committed to performing one random act of kindness every day. This filled my bucket every time. And we must give to receive, so start doing the things for others that you want to experience, and you will notice that it will come back to you tenfold. What's more, doing this without expectations will bring you the peace you seek.

Remember also that you tether yourself to whatever you put your energy into. So, when you end things, whether it is a relationship or you leave a home or a job, you need to take the time to also energetically end whatever it is you no longer want to be tethered to. This will enable you to move on cleanly and completely. Take the time to consciously end it and reclaim your energy. Reclaim your power. You can simply declare and affirm it as being so – and so it is! Or you can do a more formal ritual like a burning ceremony to release it. Either way, let it go. This will clear the space for something to enter that is more aligned with where you are at that time.

When you raise your vibration, you will feel more fulfilled, happier and lighter. You will also automatically enhance your ability to manifest and allow in what you really want. In the next chapter, we are going to a talk about how you can start to raise your receiving levels even further to actualize abundance in your life like never before.

8
ACTUALIZING ABUNDANCE

"Abundance is not something we acquire,
it's something we tune into."
—Wayne Dyer

When we are vibrating high, our manifestations come easily and effortlessly. We feel in flow with everything, and the synchronicities happen at every turn. We are in tune with abundance.

It feels magical, like you have your own wand or fairy godmother with you, and almost limitless. But it is also often short-lived. It's like we hit a ceiling that we just cannot break through. Gay Hendricks, the noted author of "The Big Leap," calls this our "upper-limit problem." It is as if we unconsciously cannot sustain or get comfortable with this next level of success or growth.

You can see this play out a lot with celebrities, professional athletes and lottery winners. It is as if they aren't ready to handle the success or fortune that has come their way, and they fall, sometimes losing it all along the way.

This is not just bad luck. This is self-sabotage. We all have an unconscious receiving level that we live into. It is much easier and more comfortable to stay with what we are familiar with than to get to the next level, no matter how much we think we want it. The why behind this is our "abundance block," which prevents us from receiving what our best selves want. We all have them, and they are formed when we are very young, sometimes through trauma but definitely through experience. Often it is just programing we absorb unknowingly from our parents or society.

ABUNDANCE BLOCKS

In order to move past where you are and live fully and abundantly into the next level, you must excavate your blocks. There are many blocks that can keep you from actualizing abundance in your life. The best place to start digging is with your money story. We all have one. And while money is not the only expression of abundance (clearly – we have been discussing higher levels of consciousness as the goal here!), money is a surrogate for worthiness in many cases. The power and story we ascribe to money is often tied to our self-worth, value and even health. Our relationship with money is usually similar to our relationship with ourselves and others as well as with our overall well-being.

Let me give you an example. One pattern around money could look like this: You make a lot but burn through it just as fast as you make it (sometimes even spending beyond your means) because you know you can always make or manifest more. The result is that you are so burned out from working hard that you spend more money on things you really don't need but that give you a hit of pleasure. You rationalize every purchase by thinking that you deserve whatever you just bought because, after all, you work really hard. The result? A vicious cycle in which you have to keep working harder to pay for more, and then you need a greater hit of pleasure or relief to keep working hard.

In this scenario, you have become a servant to your lifestyle. You are exhausted but cannot stop because you constantly need more money to manage your expenses. This was me.

Not surprisingly, this pattern carried over to other areas of my life like my ability to be on time and be truly present in my life. This, in turn, affected my relationships. I would always try to do one extra thing, multitask or cram something in before I left the house, for instance, that I would end up being late and let others down in the process – including my kids sometimes. I always ran things to the limit, from myself to my gas tank. (No kidding, I cannot tell you how many times I just made it to the gas station in time.) I was living life ragged, and I was depleted. This was not who I wanted to be, but I continued the pattern for a very long time. And that kept me from consciously staying in alignment with what I truly wanted: more ease and freedom in my life as well as to be a more grounded and present person and parent.

When you are in a cycle like this, you inevitably compromise yourself, whether it's by staying in a job you hate, working with clients that drain you or even staying in a marriage that is no longer working.

Of course, your relationship with money might look different. For instance, I once had a client who had a very fearful relationship with money. It wasn't that he didn't have enough money. By most standards, he was very wealthy. It was his fear and scarcity mindset that kept him imprisoned. He was so afraid of losing his money that he did not allow himself to enjoy it. This fear of losing it all carried over to how he operated in the world and kept him from showing up fully in his work and relationships. Once he was able to make peace with his relationship with money, he felt safe to be more vulnerable in his marriage and advocate for himself at work. His whole world shifted.

But no matter what the specifics of your money story might be, chances are that story is doing more than affecting other areas of your life. It's very likely driving your decisions entirely. When we start to unravel our beliefs around money and abundance, we can make more empowered, conscious choices that align with our higher selves and move us beyond the trappings of our old patterns. We can break through that upper-limit problem.

Knowing how much power you give money is a start, but you'll probably have to shift the way you think about it. Money, like anything else, is just energy. Those who have a lot of money don't usually think about it too much. They don't put it in the driver's seat, so to speak. Instead, they stay in a high vibration about it, expecting there to be an abundance of it and focusing their attention and energy elsewhere. I know it can seem hard to do this when you do not have as much as you would like, but acting "as if" is essential to actualizing abundance in your life.

Look at where you vibrate around money. Is it in fear? Do you feel guilty or shameful about your money or lack of money? I have actually worked with many clients who feel guilty about having too much, and this carries over to their self-perception. If they feel they are unworthy of the money they have, they tend to feel they are unworthy as human beings. An internal battle ensues in which the person spends most of their time proving to themselves and others that they deserve what they have. The ironic part is that they can't even enjoy the money they have at that point. They're just locked in an all-consuming endeavor to justify why they have what they have – and sometimes they find it slip away from them as a result.

If you allow yourself to raise your vibration around money and get to a place of acceptance, neutrality or even love around money, it will flow more easily to you. I experienced this when I manifested the insurance money after my husband's death. I have shared this story before, but it bears repeating. My insurance claim was initially rejected because my husband's death was a suicide. But every day, I visualized the money coming to me. I got in alignment with the feeling of relief it would bring by helping me and my daughters move forward. I let go of the fear and surrendered to the idea that it was coming. And it did! It arrived three months after the initial rejection. My lawyers still don't know how it happened.

Once I had that money, it was easier to live with ease. I was free to make decisions that worked for me and my girls. I did not have to stay at my job; I could do work that I loved. I could make different choices. But I also understood a deeper truth: It wasn't the money that made the difference. It was the feeling of being free.

I told myself to remember that feeling if and when a time came that I did not have as much money. There is no doubt that money can make a difference, but money is a means goal, not an end goal. What we really desire is what we think money will give us: security, safety, freedom, adventure, opportunities. To step into this level of abundance, you can begin to make choices from this place of alignment before the money actually comes. Then, when you are in a higher vibration, you will see the money begin to flow to you easily and effortlessly.

One of the things I teach my clients is how, when they make decisions, to make money in alignment with their values and who they ultimately want to be as a priority over the money itself. This is a new way of being for sure, and it can be scary at first. But I find that, once they start to put things like self-worth or freedom or adventure in the driver's seat over money, they notice a huge shift of the right thing(s) entering their world – that which is aligned with who they want to be and are becoming. And because they are on the right path and not compromising, the money flows to them too.

Now, this requires being mindful and not reckless. Living as though you have the freedom money affords you is not the same as living like a rock star (e.g., beyond your means)!

This even worked for one of my clients who is a financial advisor! I was grateful she was open to trying. By placing more importance on her values (working with people who were respectful of her and doing work that was meaningful) over just the money, she experienced a significant amount of ease in certain areas of her life including her business, which before seemed strenuous and unwavering. During our work together, she was even able to sell off a business that had been draining her for years. And she sold it for significantly more than she expected to, and faster and with more ease than she imagined possible. It was by letting go of her fears and making aligned choices that she opened the necessary space to receive what she deeply wanted.

When I work with clients, one of three beliefs around money usually emerges as the block that's preventing them from living fully into their potential and abundance.

1. That money is bad or even the "root of all evil"
2. That rich people are selfish or bad and not like them
3. That money only comes through hard work and struggle

If you are paying attention to the levels of consciousness and the vibration of these words, you can see right away how these beliefs can box you in and create a scarcity mindset. If you associate the one thing that you are wanting with being bad, evil or not for you, or you correlate pain and struggle with it, you create a low vibrational relationship with it. Furthermore, you risk possibly repelling it from yourself altogether.

Now any of these statements could apply to other areas of abundance in your life besides money, like joy, relationships, friendships, adventure and love. If you want more of something, you need to get into a heart-centered connection (a LOVE vibration) with it. You need to see it as helpful and good, to see it as something for you, and make it easy to attract. I find the first two beliefs are easier for people to reframe, but the last one is tougher. This is often because they believe all the money and abundance they have accumulated is a result of their hard work and struggle. And it's no wonder. Consider how our society teaches us that success comes from hard work. Or how we are wrapped up in busyness and being able to multitask or juggle more and more. We are so concerned about being productive that we often lose sight of our priorities and why we are doing a task or job in the first place.

So here is the mind hack to counteract all that: Replace the words "hard work and struggle" with "focused effort and ease." Start to step into the idea that your success comes from doing things in a mindful and focused way, and look for evidence of when this is true. Yes, your success takes effort, but usually we are most successful when we are operating in our zone of genius. This is actually where we can do things with ease and flow because we are operating from a place of connection with our highest strengths. When you focus in alignment with these areas, you will find less resistance and struggle and more effortless success. Continue to choose work that aligns with your zone of genius, and you will see your productivity and fulfillment soar as well as your abundance increase.

NEW NARRATIVES

Life is not a zero-sum game. An abundance mindset assumes that there is plenty to go around. The Universe is loving and generous, and when we gain or acquire something, it does not mean it came at the expense of someone else. Allowing yourself to shift from a scarcity mindset to one of abundance requires you to change your beliefs and step into a new narrative. If there is something you want for yourself, whether it is a new job, a new relationship or a spiritual path forward, you must believe it is available to you first. You have to lean into the idea that if it is open to others, it is also open to you. You may add that it is because you are a child of God, or you can just accept the idea that if it can happen for them, it can happen for you – you are one of "them" too.

At first, this may feel artificial or hard to believe, but your inner work here is to decide to believe it anyway. If you notice that what you are wanting is opening up to others around you, accept this as a sign that you are in the right circles for receiving and you are that much closer. Do not fall victim to the mind's deception that it is already taken and no longer for you. In fact, the opposite is happening. Envy is a very low vibration. Reframe that thought immediately and use it as a means for clarity. What you are envious about is just pointing you to what you truly want. Give thanks to the Universe for reminding you and move on.

Comparison is a mind trap. Do not fall for its seductiveness. You are on the path you are meant to be on, and at the right place at the right time. No one else has experienced what you have the way you have, and so of course your timing and path forward will be different. When you find yourself in the low vibration of comparison, which is, at best, vibrating around pride or anger and, at worst, shame-based, remind yourself this is not for you. As Hawkins' research revealed, whenever you are vibrating below the line of courage (a low vibration), your body muscle tests in a weakened state, which means that the emotions you are experiencing are not aligned with your truth. Elevate your thoughts into gratitude and appreciation for where you are now, and for how far you have come, and give thanks for what is next for you.

Gratitude is a tool to lift you out of any scarcity situation and help open up your receiving levels. In "Know

What You Want Next," I talk a lot about the importance of gratitude and how it shifted my way of being and living. Having a gratitude practice is an essential component of staying in a high vibrational state. Bookending your days with gratitude is a way to stay mindful, but extending that to the things you want also helps you manifest them faster. When you move gratitude into the present moment, it is as if something has already arrived. Act as if by affirming yes, thank you for this beautiful home, the clarity I seek, the blessing for my family, etc. Claim that it is here, and savor it in the energy in which you want to receive it. See how quickly it comes to you.

NEW BEHAVIORS

Just as you elevate your thoughts around abundance, so too must you shift your actions and behaviors. Remember aligned action? You must follow that regarding your new abundance mindset. This requires that you act in alignment with what you believe to be true about what you are worthy of receiving. Start to become more mindful of how you spend your time and energy. Start substituting the working hard and struggling with slowing down and focusing with ease and flow. This is how to begin. Instead of multitasking your way through the day, which is in essence scattering undirected energy all over the place, mindfully focus on one thing at a time.

This is essential for getting into an elevated state. You must have resonance with what you want, and if you are focused on three to five things at a time, nothing receives your full attention. When you do stuff on autopilot, so to speak, you are essentially not paying attention. You are ignoring the thing you actually want. Focus on one thing at a time, give it your care and see how it starts to take shape. Bring the vibration of what you want to live into to that task, and notice how it shifts the energy and brings more of that vibration to you. A simple example of this is making a lunch for someone. When you take the time and care to put a little love into it, people feel that. Slow down and be deliberate in the vibration you want to be in. Give and you shall receive. Remind yourself how blessed you are to have those in your life to care for.

You must also keep your side of the street clean. What I mean by this is loose ends and unfinished business are abundance blocks. Avoiding unpaid bills, unopened emails, lingering conversations or difficult tasks prevents you from allowing in what you want in your life. You will notice this quickly with simple things like payments. If you are sitting on paying a bill, you will soon enough find yourself on the receiving end of that. One of your clients or someone you know who owes you money might hold off payment the way you did with someone or something else. Pay that bill and notice how quickly you receive the money in your hands.

If you are feeling stuck in your energy work or with manifesting, take an inventory of any unfinished business or cluttered space in your life. Start taking deliberate action to shift the energy by settling each item. You will begin to feel unencumbered and lighter. Your vibration will actually begin to elevate just by performing these simple actions, which create energetic space for what you want to receive.

If you have a habit of procrastination or avoiding things or doing things at the last minute, get curious about this. Most likely this is fear-based. What are you making up about this? Reframe your narrative around it by giving gratitude for what it will bring you or how you will feel once it is completed. This goes for paying bills, too (Again, money is usually the biggest block.) If you avoid paying bills until the last minute, look at it this way: Instead of focusing on the loss of money (scarcity) as you write the check or transfer the money, focus on the gratitude you have for what it is you are paying for – the ability to live in a beautiful home, to provide electricity and heat for your family, for that amazing vacation and memories. Again, money is just a means goal. Shift your attention to the end goal and give thanks for it.

Lastly, I want to leave you with this idea. Money is currency. Money is energy. It is meant to flow. Do not fear allowing it to do its job. Trust when you give it away and allow it to flow. Do not cling to it out of fear, but rather respect it and give it care and spend with intention and gratitude; it will flow back to you. Start to develop a new relationship with money, or any area of abundance in your life that is not flowing, and you will see a dramatic shift. Add a money mantra to your ritual, like "I am grateful that money flows to me from many different sources with ease." Experiment with these shifts and see how you quickly you raise your receiving level and lower your fears around money.

Greater abundance blocks may also exist within your interpersonal relationships. Making amends, forgiving and letting go of burdens are necessary to get yourself to the next level in that realm. As we discussed before, closure and releasing any stagnant or negative energy is necessary for creating the space to allow in what you are wanting and for elevating you forward. Creating daily rituals where you scan yourself for emotional blocks and clear them energetically, and where you mentally choose which vibration you want to live into, will keep you in an upward spiral.

As you release one abundance block, you may discover a new one. This is lifelong work: We are never done growing or ascending. Accept that as a normal part of the process and know that you are on the right track.

9
RECOVERING FROM TRIGGERS, PITFALLS AND FREEFALLS

"There's no situation we can't make peace with."
—Byron Katie

Our journey toward elevation and soul growth is not a linear one. As you hit a new edge or level, you will bump up against old patterns and new challenges. Setting the course ahead with these expectations will help you on your way forward. I often joke with my clients that if you want to find out just how enlightened you really are, see how Thanksgiving goes with your siblings. No matter how conscious you are, you will still get triggered from time to time, and being with your family of origin can be the greatest test of your conscious prowess. Remind yourself it is all about how quickly you the recover from your triggers and how you react.

The best way to manage triggers is to have a reframe ready for them. That assumes you know your triggers already, like we discussed in Chapter 4. The trigger itself is the bad stuff, and how you manage it is where your power of choice comes in. Will you choose to be courageous enough to go higher into an above-the-line vibration? Or, will you fall into a lower vibration and channel your ugly Inner Medusa? Knowing that you always have all parts of you available to you, it is good to practice for such situations ahead of time.

If you know that you are going into a situation that may awaken your Inner Medusa, make a conscious choice ahead of time about how you choose to be in those circumstances. Commit to being your higher self beforehand, and get really clear on what that looks like as well as how you'll respond when you're inevitably triggered. Reframe your default pattern by embodying the traits of your higher self, and making it your goal to stick to that no matter what. This means you need to put your ego and inner child in check before you enter the arena, so to speak.

When you allow yourself to relax into this new way of being, you will also find that you do not need so much armor, that you feel safe just being your authentic self.

The need to be right, or be seen/heard, or be the prettiest/ brightest in the room, or play your old role in the family will no longer drive you. Instead, you will mindfully choose to be your best self.

Having a more empowered thought or goal to consciously focus on in the moment will also keep you grounded when you get triggered. For instance, if you are going into a situation where you are afraid of the judgment of others or fearful you may "fail," remind yourself ahead of time that this thought might come up, and have another story handy to replace it with. Focus on a time when you did shine and did succeed, and people embraced you. Embody this experience and let yourself return to this memory when and if a triggered thought comes up.

Admittedly, this is not easy as being triggered is often a visceral experience. So, how do you counteract that to stay grounded in your higher self? This is my Reframe Formula:

1. **Recognize** it for what it is – an old wound from your past and not the truth in this current moment.

2. **Refocus** yourself by pausing and taking three deep breaths to shut off the fight-or-flight response within you.

3. **Reframe** your attention on embodying your higher self – do what your inner goddess, inner leader or inner warrior would do in that situation.

Priming yourself daily to embody your higher self in your thoughts, actions and behaviors can help build the necessary resiliency for when you do feel like you are being attacked and want to avoid being hijacked by a lower vibration.

Sometimes you will do great and sometimes you won't. That is OK. That is human. Your job is to keep noticing, keep learning and keep returning to your higher self. And remember to stay in a high vibration. You must also give yourself that unconditional love and kindness you would show someone else. These moments when you slip actually help your evolution. You get stronger with each fall and learn to handle it with more grace the next time. Keep moving along and resist dwelling on your setbacks. What's more, have compassion for the work you are doing and celebrate your wins along the way. By savoring those moments, they will start to take up more space within you than the missteps, and that will help you continue moving upward.

What if you have a big free fall down the shame well? Don't worry. It will happen … and it's OK. You just need a plan for what to do next. We all have our trip down the well at some point. It is just not a place where we want to stay. Let yourself process the emotion. Let it move through you. Feel it, notice it, breathe through it and mindfully let it go. When you are ready to climb back out, anchor yourself in the present moment. Notice which emotion takes over. What are you feeling? Where are you vibrating? Once you know where you are residing energetically, you can start to elevate higher. You may need to process different emotions on your ascension – in the moment or over time – with whatever life throws you. This is your real-life work. You are learning how to become the master of yourself.

When I want to rise out of a slump, the first thing I do is return to love by connecting into my heart center. I allow myself to get present and stay grounded in the pink light. I let it wash over me and envelop me like a warm hug. I focus on this present moment and mindfully catch myself when I drift out of this state.

During 2020, this was a frequent practice for myself and for my clients. When fear was so omnipresent, I would remind myself that, in that present moment, I was safe. I was healthy. My family was safe. My family was healthy. We were doing everything to stay healthy. We were doing everything to stay safe. This helped me to let go of the fear and bring my attention instead to the truth of what was there and then.

Choosing to live in the moment and be present is a way to alleviate fears and silence the what-ifs and worst-case scenarios that can play in our heads. Following up with some self-care or helping others can further raise your state of being. If we can turn our attention away from our fears and ourselves and towards something bigger, we can start disrupting those neural pathways. This applies also to the fear around doing something out of your comfort zone. If you can focus on why you are doing it and make it about that – almost depersonalize it – it lets the fear of judgment or failure start to slip away. It is bigger than you and not about you.

When I work with entrepreneurs this comes up a lot, especially when they are trying to get over the fear of putting themselves out there. When they go back to their "why," their purpose, it gives them more courage and the fear subsides.

Recovering From Triggers, Pitfalls and freefalls

One of the biggest game changers is to turn our attention away from ourselves and be of genuine humble service. When we are stuck in shame or guilt or even pride, the best way to disrupt this is to do something for someone else. Choose to go to a place of unconditional kindness (joy) and notice how quickly you not only return to yourself but feel an inner upward shift. So much of our unhappiness and apathy comes from focusing on ourselves too much and not being connected to others or being part of something bigger. Low vibrations are self-absorbed, even emotions like grief and guilt. When we can consciously choose to move into connection with others, we start to feel the spark of inner joy and ultimately peace.

Always return to the idea that you are at choice with how you want to be. This is how you can instantly empower yourself. Choose to vibrate above the line at courage. You can do this by focusing on what you can control and not getting lost in the chaos around you. Research shows that only 10% of our happiness is driven by our circumstances, so you have a lot of room for choice. Once you rise out of a lower vibration up to courage, you can rise further.

Here are some helpful reframes that can empower you to shift out of a lower vibration and get to the next level – and ultimately back to being above the line.

Emotion	Reframe/Mantra/Action
Pride/Stuck in Your Ego	Be humble. Go within and sit in silence. Meditate/pray.
Anger	Channel anger through exercise Choose to forgive. Let go.
Desire	Focus on working on yourself instead of being at the mercy of external factors for change. Affirm: "I am whole as I am."
Grief	Choose to live in the present. Accept. Surrender. Move forward.
Apathy	Choose hope. Ask for and accept help. Take action – get moving. Do something active to move stagnant energy.
Guilt/Blame	Have self-compassion. Take responsibility for your part and affirm: "I forgive myself."

Shame	Honor your self-worth. Tell yourself, "I am enough; I am worthy." Choose life. Help someone else. Shift your focus away from yourself and recognize your value by helping others.
Fear	Be in the present moment. Affirm: "I am safe." Choose faith in life/God. Live in the now moment.

Now, just as there are triggers, there are things that can tempt you and hook your ego into a lower state even if you are otherwise vibrating high. Things that can bring us back down to ego may appear to be positive – like fame and fortune, for instance. However, what drives the fame and fortune is key. Is it a result of you being authentic and genuine, or is it coming from a place of pride? This is an important discernment. I have witnessed some of my most successful clients experience this internal struggle. The best way to deal with this is to bring yourself back to the question: Is this serving my soul or my ego? Then let your soul guide you and take aligned action.

You may also get hooked by desire, whether that's for material things or a relationship. You can feel this hook in your body. I used to feel this way about clothes. I had to have the latest and greatest for each season. I would scan the internet looking for the perfect outfit, and when I found it, I had to have it! I could feel myself get lost in the thrill of it. This was fun, but it was not a grounded place to be. Once I left the corporate world, my need for clothes, shoes and stuff started to dissipate. I did not need those things as much to satisfy me or to justify my choices. The key here is to pause and recenter yourself. Detach from that hooked emotion, create mental space for yourself and then reassess what you want. Is it still something you want or need, or were you just getting hooked in the moment? Giving yourself 24 hours is always a good idea.

The 24-hour rule is good for really anything that hooks or triggers you. Hit pause. Sit on that email. Hold off on responding. Sleep on it. Return to it tomorrow. Choose consciously. Trust. Repeat. You got this!

10
FINDING YOUR FLOW

"Everything that is meant for you will find a way."
—Unknown

I f you've lived for any length of time, chances are you've encountered some adversity along the way. And it's equally likely then that you've come across a deceptively simple phrase with layers of meaning: This too shall pass. When you are in a difficult situation, grieving or experiencing a loss of some sort, it is extremely hard to fathom that this state of being you are presently in is temporary. I remember when I lost my husband, I never thought that feeling of dread would pass. But eventually … it did. And yes, recovering from grief does take time, but I believe we have more power than just waiting for time to pass. When we allow ourselves to be with, to let go, to *flow* with what is here now, things move faster and often with more ease.

Everything is indeed temporary. This is why it is so important to savor the good times while we are in them by being fully present. Life ebbs and flows. There is no way to hold onto one particular state of being at all times, unless you are immune to being human. Instead, we need to learn to surrender to the flow while being mindful in the process.

What do I mean by this? Well, as you move through your life, allow yourself to feel all the feels. Let the emotions move through you fully and then let them go. Remind yourself that the quickest way to move through the pain, conflict and grief is to feel it. Our bodies, our minds and our spirits are equipped to handle anything that life may throw at us. Allow the emotion to do its job and trust that, just as quickly as the experience or feeling came, it will move on. Practice this way of being and see how much relief you feel in allowing emotions to move through you. Once they do move through you, bring yourself back to choice.

When we start to make peace with the idea that nothing is permanent, it allows us to be more open to uncertainty and the ultimate plan God or the Universe has for us. The plan that we perhaps even chose before we were born. The ebb and flow of one life is not the same as anyone else's. We are on our own spiritual paths, and each path will narrow and expand in the timing in which it is meant to. We are not in a race with anyone else. Everything that is meant for us will find us. We do not need to force it or get frustrated by how long it takes.

If we can settle into the truth of this notion, we can start to focus more on staying in a higher level of consciousness. The state of flow exists above the line of courage. This is a state where we need to let go of our attachment to the way things should be or how we expect them to be. Learning to accept our life path and who we are – the good, the bad and the ugly (and the magnificent) – is an essential first step. When we compare ourselves to others and their journey, it truly wastes our time because none of us are on the same journey. Surrendering to the idea that, yes, everything in your life you have experienced for a reason may be a difficult pill to swallow sometimes, but there is a lot of freedom when you make peace with this idea.

This is not to say life isn't hard or even unfair at times, but challenges and hardships shape us while forging the path to bring us where we are today. Think about it: If like really does attract like, and we wholeheartedly believe in the law of attraction, then in order to do your dharma or purpose in this world, you must move through hard times so that you can help those who follow behind you. I am deeply aware of the fact that my journey through loss has prepared me to do the work I am doing in the world. Is it the ultimate path I would have chosen? Probably not. But is it mine? Absolutely. And yours is yours.

The first level of acceptance is with yourself. Staying in this place of radical self-acceptance will help you to stay above the line of courage and remain in flow. Practicing self-compassion and self-care as a necessity, not a nicety, will help this stick.

Once you are able to relax into acceptance of your path, you will have more room for acceptance of others, even if they are dramatically different than you. Moving up to a level of neutrality in your state of consciousness will allow a level of empathy for others to burst open. You will find that you are just unattached from the preconceived notions, judgments or even energy of gossip in your field. You will notice your tolerance for others and their differences, whether political or religious or anything in between, will not matter as much to you. Instead, you begin to see people on a soul level.

Finding Your Flow

This is important. You cannot be an enlightened individual if you continue to judge or condemn others. (Even if you're judging and condemning silently and in your heart. In fact, especially not then.) As you start to learn to be more conscious and mindful, you must humble yourself by remembering that you were not always this way. Continue the process of looking in the mirror at what must shift in you so that you open yourself up to more acceptance and unconditional love and kindness. (Elevating to a state of love and unconditional kindness cannot, by definition, be conditional. This is why so many cannot flow in these waters.)

Just as we discussed letting an emotion move through you, allow the judgments you hold toward others to move through you. Return to love and kindness and find something about that person or group of people to empathize with. Get curious and let go of the assumptions you make. It is through neutrality of understanding that we all can rise and flow. Expand your vision, not your judgment.

As you find others on your path ahead of you, resist feeling discouraged at how far you have to go. Let their success inspire rather than deter you. Try seeking mentors and those who are in circles of states of being that you want to be in. Just be sure to look beyond the superficial layer of what they are doing and achieving to who they are and how they act. Then ask yourself, *What is it that I admire about them? Is it coming from an ego place or from my truth?* (Muscle test it if you are unsure.) Consciously evaluating who you associate with and learn from will help you to stay in alignment with who you want to be so that you can take proper action from that state of being.

It can be tempting to follow the fame, fortune and materialism that the gifts of ego success can bring, but be sure you are not seduced away from your higher path forward.

You will notice as you continue on your journey that people, situations and circumstances will fall in and out of your life. As long as you are in a higher vibrational state, allow it. It is again happening for you, not to you. There was a funny meme I saw recently that said, "God removed them from your life because he heard conversations you didn't." Trust the process of life.

As you move into a higher state, things that are not for you will fall away. Just as I was writing this book, a long-term client of mine unexpectedly discontinued our work together. At first, I was confused and frustrated. But when I allowed the emotions to move through me,

I realized that it was for the highest good of all. We were moving in different directions and were no longer flowing together. I trust in the Universe to fill the space with a more conscious fit, and I am allowing it in with divine time. I was not always this trusting in the divine process of things. Years ago, something like losing a client could have sent me down the shame well to a place of despair. But through practice and deep faith, I have learned that God always provides what is meant for the highest good of all.

Deepening your connection to God or the Universe or Source Energy – whatever you believe – will help you to find your flow as a safe and comforting place to be and will help you stay grounded in your higher self. When we trust in something bigger than ourselves, it provides us peace and a knowing that all is right in our world.

This was one of the biggest lessons I experienced during the pandemic. To alleviate my fears or worry, returning to my spiritual practice enabled me to stay more grounded and at peace even though the world around me was chaotic and confusing. I am not saying I did not fall out of flow. I did – many times! But when I did, I had an anchor to return to. (Many times!)

Mihalyi Csikszentmihalyi is one of the pioneers on the research of flow. In his book, "Flow," he describes flow as being consciously in inner harmony with whatever you're doing. I find this flow in meditation, when I dance and when I write. I can feel my soul come alive. I can feel Spirit move through me, whether that's me actually channeling or just feeling the abundance of joy within my soul. Knowing and practicing daily these bursts of inner harmony and joy will help you maintain that state of flow in your daily life. Aligning your work in the world to be in the sweet spot of what ignites your flow will help you to spend more of your waking hours in this state too. This state of flow is a place where you feel inspired and challenged but not overwhelmed.

You don't have to wait for flow to find you. You can find flow by creating it.

11
UPLEVELING

"Every uplevel in life needs a different you."
—Unknown

We are always becoming, evolving and moving forward. As we move to different edges and places in our lives and prepare for what is next, that next level will continue to require a new you. Why? Because, as you consciously move up to each level, you'll notice that more and more of your "normal" living just doesn't fit anymore. The more you go inward, the more you may feel that the external world doesn't quite vibe with where you are.

You will notice this in simple ways. Perhaps you will feel less need for material things. Or, while you appreciate beauty, you may find it more often in nature and experiences than in the shopping mall. Simplifying your life will take on more of your attention; superficiality will resonate less with you. You might begin to crave deeper conversations and more soulful connections, and you will notice how quickly the Universe provides them as if they are there for the asking. Synchronicities and chance meetings, meanwhile, uplevel with you.

You may also be feeling a deep level of gratitude and fulfillment on your current path. That is normal too. Keep allowing this experience to flourish and lean into the idea that you are being intuitively guided as you encounter any fears on your path. Life is feeling abundant, in flow and limitless as long as you swim in the waters of appreciation and mindfulness. As you focus your energy, your life flows with ease to what you are creating. It feels like everything is moving in the right direction, even if you are not 100% sure where it is going. This is how life is meant to be. This experience and knowing are precisely what will keep you moving onward and upward. Keep trusting and staying in a heart-centered vibration.

Becoming less and less attached to the ways things "should be" or how you expect them to be is essential as you uplevel. The more we cling to what we think the outcome has to be or, worse, try to force it, the more we lose our ground. Ease into the belief that everything is working out for your highest good, and stay in aligned action with what you want to receive. When you fall out of this intention, return as quickly as you can. And remember what you wanted or asked for may not look exactly how you imagined. It may be bigger or better or even unfamiliar. Get curious about it, and I am sure you will notice it is even more aligned than you could have designed. This is the power of the Universe at work.

And, even if you don't know it yet, by doing the work outlined in this book, you have been slowly unplugging from the mainstream matrix of our world. You are unraveling and undoing the years of programming that you've been fed from the Western world, society, the media and even your family. When you look to your inner truth for the answers and really trust your body, soul and intuition, you depend less on the outside world for answers and guidance. As you wake up, you may find yourself questioning what is around. It may seem to make less and less sense as you grow more connected to your authentic truth.

This process is normal. The modern world is full of falsehoods, propaganda and manufactured fear. When you are vibrating above this level of consciousness, even though it is everywhere around you, it cannot reach you – unless you let it. It is as though you now have your own invisible cloak like Harry Potter. You can consciously shut out the noise and walk through it all untouched and unscathed.

Some of what you observe may be confronting and difficult to accept. Our work is to listen deeply beyond the chaos of the world and to develop trust within ourselves for discernment and to take aligned action despite what's going on.

Now, put your hand on your heart center, take a deep breath and exhale. Notice the thoughts, emotions and sensations in your body. Take another deep breath — and acknowledge yourself for the growth and ascension you have already experienced. You have come so far.

And now sense and choose to connect to that part of you that absolutely knows your truth. Enjoy this moment as even a spark of clarity arrives. From here, let me ask you a question – one that, moment by moment, you'll ask yourself as you choose to uplevel: "At which level of consciousness do you choose to live?"

Here's to your brave journey ahead!

REFERENCES

Brennan, Barbara. "Hands of Light: A Guide to Healing Through the Human Energy Field." Bantam Books, Random House Publishing. 1987.

Hawkins, David. "Power vs. Force: The Hidden Determinants of Human Behavior." Hay House. 1995.

Hawkins, David. "Transcending the Levels of Consciousness: The Stairway to Enlightenment." Hay House. 2006.

Hendricks, Gay. "The Big Leap: Conquer Your Hidden Fear and Take Life to the Next Level." New York: Harper Collins Publisher. 2009.

Hetherington, Michael. "The Art of Self Muscle Testing." Australia: Michael Hetherington. 2013.

Napier, Kimberly. "Know What You Want Next." Boston: Washington Franklin Publishing. 2019.

Nemeth, Maria. "The Energy of Money: A Spiritual Guide to Financial and Personal Fulfillment." Random House Publishing Group. 1997.

ABOUT THE AUTHOR

Kimberly Napier is a certified life and business coach, bestselling author and intuitive medium who helps women create lives and businesses they love and that are infused with meaning and fulfillment.

Kimberly found this calling after a tragic wake-up call that propelled her to design a new life for herself and her daughters. Prior to coaching, Kimberly led a successful, 22-year corporate career in marketing research where she helped shape the "purpose" behind some of the country's most iconic consumer brands. Now she leverages her expertise to guide women in unleashing *their* purpose in the world.

Kimberly has helped hundreds of women cultivate the clarity and courage to live personally and professionally empowered on their terms. In addition to her coaching practice, Kimberly leads global retreats and online courses, and she spearheads a Mastermind Class for Women Entrepreneurs.

She is the author of "Know What You Want Next: Break Free of the 'I Don't Know' Trap and Love Your Life Again" and "Elevated: Take Your Life to the Next Level." She is also the co-host of the podcast, *Manifesting Mastery*.

Kimberly holds an MBA from Babson College, is certified in positive psychology and is a Professional Certified Coach (PCC) with The International Coaching Federation. She received her coaching training though the Co-Active Training Institute (CTI). She has also trained in reiki, akashic records and mediumship with world-renowned teachers. Kimberly lives outside of Boston with her husband, four children and two golden retrievers.

You can learn more and connect with Kimberly at kimberlynapier.com.